# "IT WAS ON FIRE WHEN I LAST CHECKED ON IT,"

## THE EASY COOKBOOK FOR VERY BUSY WOMEN

Robin Soslow

Illustrations by Joe Azar

# ACKNOWLEDGEMENTS

I'd like to thank these people for their wit, wisdom and support: Bill Cates and Rich Lippman; Dennis Goris, who designed this book; Alice Catchings, Sandy Coleman, Candy Griffin, Patti Joseph, Tamara Kirson, Mike Linowes, Buena Peacock, John Rankin, Ellen Schindler, Lynne Scrimgeour, Lori Skrobola, Mason Smawley, Carolyn Smith, Kevin Tierney, Juliet Ward, Betsy Young; my folks Janet and Irv; and to my friends who sampled, savored and survived my culinary creations.

## Copy Editors & Test Kitchens

CorkScrew Press would also like to thank these brave individuals for their gracious assistance, editing skills and intestinal fortitude:

Ro & Shel, Joe Cates, Leslie Bloom, Winafred Brantl, Bonnie Buchanan, Karen Cuppett, Donna Dalaski, Liz Engdahl, E. Erik Evenson (drink consultant and author of *The Shooter Book*), Betsy Franklin, Jane Garmon, Monica Goldberg, Robert Luskin (wine consultant), Trina Meyer, Erin McCormick, Larry McGhee, Christine Nichols, Mary Anna Portner, Margie Schwartz, Mary Schaff, Judy Traub, Terrie Upshur, Kathy Welch, Karen Gruber and Natalie Windsor.

Cover design by Donna Panullo

CorkScrew Press

4470-107 Sunset Blvd., Suite 234
Los Angeles, CA 90027

Text Copyright ©1991 by Robin Soslow
Illustrations Copyright ©1991 by Joe Azar

Portions of this book previously appeared in *The Official Single Woman's Cookbook* by Robin Soslow.

Distributed in Canada by Firefly Books, Ltd., 250 Sparks Ave., Willowdale, Ontario M2H 2S4

Trademarks used in this book are property of various trademark owners.

ISBN 0-944042-08-2
Library of Congress Number 91-072486

Printed in the U.S.A.

10 9 8 7 6 5 4 3 2 1

To order more copies of this book, and *EATING IN—The Official Single Man's Cookbook*, see page 143.

# TO:

## BUSY WOMEN
ready to kiss Kitchen Performance Anxiety goodbye . . .

## THEIR STARVING MATES
who hunger for a self-actualized woman who can really cook . . .

## THEIR BEWILDERED FRIENDS
who wonder how *anyone* can survive on microwave popcorn . . .

## AND THEIR ANXIOUS PARENTS
who stare helplessly at the sight of their daughters' kitchens . . .

## *HERE IS YOUR SECRET INGREDIENT!*

# *Busy women discover the pleasures of becoming born-again cooks:*

*"MY HUSBAND USED TO DO ALL THE COOKING, and let everyone in the world know it. Now, I get the credit, and he gets to do the dishes."*

*—P.M., psychologist*

*"FOR OUR FIRST DATE, HE ACTUALLY COOKED a fantastic dinner! But I didn't dare return the invitation for fear I'd poison him. Now, thanks to your easy recipes, he keeps coming back for seconds."*

*—S.L., biologist*

*"MY FOLKS STOPPED NAGGING ME every time they visited. Now they even ask for doggie bags!"*

*—K.S., actress*

*"I DREADED COOKING FOR MY OFFICE PARTIES. So did my office. But not anymore!"*

*—J.R., association executive*

*"I THOUGHT I HAD IT ALL. A great career. Big salary. Uptown apartment. And Mr. Right. But the first time I cooked for him, he threw up his hands and bolted out the door. Where was your book when I needed it?"*

*—D.W., attorney*

*"I WAS ALWAYS TOO BUSY TO COOK. That's why I love this cookbook—I can always find something that's fast, easy and tastes great."*

*—P.B., real estate agent*

# "IT WAS ON FIRE

# WHEN I LAST CHECKED ON IT."

### THE EASY COOKBOOK
### FOR VERY BUSY WOMEN

## About The Author

ROBIN SOSLOW used to endure biting remarks like, "Just bring the paper cups"..."Your specialty should bear a Surgeon General's Warning"...and "Weren't you a poster child for *Bon Appetit?*" Now she hears, "You must give me the recipe!"..."Let me be your guinea pig!" and, "Will you marry me?"

## About The Illustrator

JOE AZAR learned a lot about cooking—and single women—after illustrating *EATING IN—The Official Single Man's Cookbook*. This new book is drawn from his experiences. Now he simply hands it to all the women who expect him to do the cooking...

# Table of Contents

Conquer Your KPA
Page 16

Dinner Dos & Don'ts
Page 27

Sweet Sinsations
Page 88

## SECTION IV—FEEDING THE FOLKS

Steamy Soups
Page 57

Common Cooking Disorders
Page 17

CHAPTER 1

# Conquering KPA*

*The Superwoman's
Final Frontier*

*t*alk about performance anxiety!

As women of the '90s, we face it every day. We're expected to excel in the boardroom, the bedroom and every room in between. We're expected to keep up with the latest fads, keep ahead of the competition, and keep our minds, bodies and homes in top shape.

Now, we Superwomen find ourselves in another domain where we're expected to shine. The Kitchen.

And baby, it's a jungle in there.

Sure, back in the days of bra-burning, ERA and sex 'n' drugs 'n' rock 'n' roll it was cool not to cook. But since then, we've endured Yuppies, The Sensitive Male and New Age music. And today, cooking has been elevated from domestic drudgery to a fine art. Being lame in the kitchen is no longer a political statement. It's a social handicap.

Truth is, the importance of earning your MBA, being elected to the Board of Directors or sweeping the tennis tournament can fade fast if the office grapevine is buzzing with jokes about your potluck creations. Or when you can't get Mr. Right over to your place for dinner.

Well, take heart. You're holding the book that will help you overcome Kitchen Performance Anxiety and achieve results that cost less than therapy. . .last longer than new lingerie. . .and satisfy you more than any other self-help technique. In short, you'll learn how to cook smart, not hard.

***Kitchen Performance Anxiety**

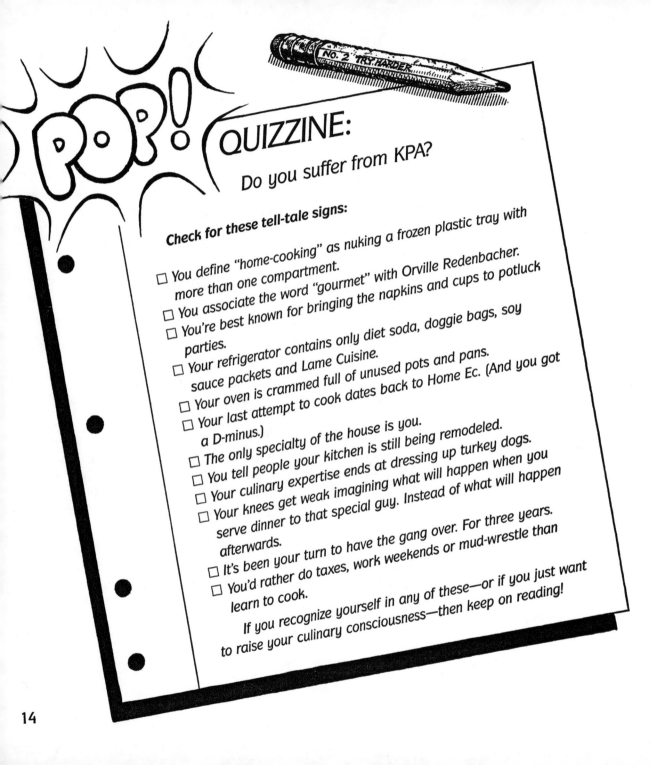

# POP!

# QUIZZINE:

## Do you suffer from KPA?

**Check for these tell-tale signs:**

☐ You define "home-cooking" as nuking a frozen plastic tray with more than one compartment.

☐ You associate the word "gourmet" with Orville Redenbacher.

☐ You're best known for bringing the napkins and cups to potluck parties.

☐ Your refrigerator contains only diet soda, doggie bags, soy sauce packets and Lame Cuisine.

☐ Your oven is crammed full of unused pots and pans.

☐ Your last attempt to cook dates back to Home Ec. (And you got a D-minus.)

☐ The only specialty of the house is you.

☐ You tell people your kitchen is still being remodeled.

☐ Your culinary expertise ends at dressing up turkey dogs.

☐ Your knees get weak imagining what will happen when you serve dinner to that special guy. Instead of what will happen afterwards.

☐ It's been your turn to have the gang over. For three years.

☐ You'd rather do taxes, work weekends or mud-wrestle than learn to cook.

If you recognize yourself in any of these—or if you just want to raise your culinary consciousness—then keep on reading!

### How did you become a stranger in your own kitchen?

- You were a sheltered child. Your mother didn't want her daughter wasting time on domestic chores when she should be studying law, medicine or business.

- You don't have a cooking expert to rely on. Mom's too nosy. Granny's mind wanders. And your friends are fast food junkies.

- You're afraid of your kitchen. You associate it with hot, smoke-belching monsters, nasty burns and big let-downs that trigger traumatic memories of ex-boyfriends.

- Your kitchen skills have atrophied. For years you've been fixing him the same ol' meatloaf and mashed potatoes whenever you get around to cooking. And besides, you'd rather spend your free time swinging a racquet than a spatula.

Whatever the reasons for your kitchen hang-ups, this book will take you from inept to adept—and help you create magnificent meals with no major ordeals.

*One early cause of KPA:*
*Mom encouraged you to play doctor rather than play house.*

## Why you should conquer your KPA.

**Better Health.** Maybe what you thought was your biological clock ticking was really your stomach growling. Think about this next time you're in some restaurant picking at your tasteless diet plate or peeling a soggy roll off a greasy burger. It's time to take control of your diet—and your life.

**Self-Sufficiency.** Do you feel like a guest in your own kitchen? Not at home on the range? Do you rate a reserved table at the nearest BurgerThing. . .and your own lane at the drive-thru window? Now you can replace kitchen mystery with mastery.

**A Competitive Edge.** Your guest (or victim) is probably comparing your cooking to his mom's, his ex's, the Other Woman's—or his own, which may be pretty darn good. Now you'll never worry about being outcooked and outclassed again.

**Your Love Life.** A man can't live on love alone. We're not advocating antiquated social attitudes, but let's face it—cooking remains a key tactical skill in the game of love.

## The end to one-night stands. The start of a lasting love affair.

Make your hungry dinner companion stop begging for mercy—and start begging for more! Just follow these tips, techniques and time-tested recipes for mutually gratifying dinners.

And because you'll actually discover much more satisfaction in cooking than you ever imagined, you'll also find some mean cuisine to impress your friends, your folks, his folks and your co-workers.

Yes, you too can conquer Kitchen Performance Anxiety. Just open up and say "ahhh!"

# Do you suffer from any Common Cooking Disorders?

## Here's how to free yourself of these bad habits without getting burned.

### Herbes (a/k/a Spice Abuse)

*Symptom:* Promiscuous, indiscriminate over-seasoning.

*Cure:* Plug holes in spice jars with toothpicks.

### Chocoholism

*Symptoms:* Chipless chocolate chip cookies, missing centers from Tootsie Roll Pops, closet M&M popping, frequent pilgrimages to Hershey, PA.

*Cure:* Confine chocoholic in a padded room with a case of unsweetened Baker's chocolate squares.

### Batter Splatter

*Symptoms:* Splattered walls, ceilings, pets and guests from lack of batter control.

*Cure:* Pitch a tent in kitchen and wear a batter-proof vest.

### Bowlimia

*Symptom:* Compulsive licking of batter-coated bowls.

*Cure:* Pepper the bowls with cayenne before licking.

### Pan-o-wrexia

*Symptom:* Absent-minded burning of cookware.

*Cure:* Strap timer to victim's wrist (with loud alarm, smoke detector and shock buzzer).

### Mono-nuke-leosis

*Symptom:* Cooking the same kind of microwave entree day after day after day.

*Cure:* Weld freezer door shut and give victim this book.

### Conspicuous Consumption

*Symptom:* Uncontrollable binging in public places.

*Cure:* Chew gum flavored with Crazy Glue.

17

# Just Say "NO" To These Unfit Substitutions

*Caution:* As with men, looks can be deceiving

MEAT TENDERIZER

SPATULA

GARLIC PRESS

TONGS

CORER & PARER

VEGETABLE BRUSH

ROLLING PIN

TURKEY BASTER

POTATO PEELER

CORN SILKER

PASTRY BRUSH

DESSERT TOPPING

SCOURING PAD

ONION HOLDER

18

# CHAPTER 2

# Let's Go On a Pantry Raid!

### (Or Don't Get Caught With Your Pans Down)

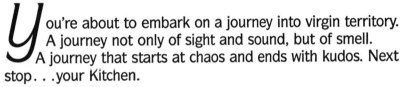

ou're about to embark on a journey into virgin territory. A journey not only of sight and sound, but of smell. A journey that starts at chaos and ends with kudos. Next stop. . .your Kitchen.

Take a deep breath. Go to your refrigerator. Fling open the door.

Ick—is that a petri dish from biology class? Yuck—what's that fuzzy green stuff? Gross—is that Chinese take-out from the Ming Dynasty? Strap on your surgical mask and toss 'em.

Next, scope out your cabinets. Hmmmm. Hot Dog Helper. Tater Tatters. NeuterSweet. Minute Mush. MSG. STP. Phony Phood. Do you have health insurance? Life insurance? Who's your next of kin?

Now, break out your cooking gear. Are you still waiting for someone to throw you a kitchen shower? Look, stuck to the shelf—it's a monster cookbook—unabridged, unreadable and unused. (Keep it on hand as a step stool.)

Time to make a fresh start! Take the Master Chef Shopping List to the nearest department and grocery stores. You're going to accessorize your kitchen correctly and get what you want: Good food. Great health. And glowing praise from family, friends and that poor starving man of yours.

# *Throw Yourself A Kitchen Shower!*

Use the list below to assemble your kitchen ensemble. Unlike shopping for your wardrobe, you'll probably buy some things you can use over and over again. And these classics will never go out of style.

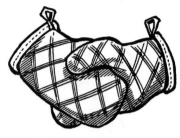

*2 oven mitts*

## Master Chef Shopping List: *Hardware*

*10" diameter non-stick
frying pan & lid*

*8" chef's knife*

*4" paring knife*

*5-quart pot & lid*

*Garlic press*

*Serrated bread knife*

*Plastic slotted
flat spatula*

*Plastic slotted
spoon*

*Measuring spoons*

*Grater*

*1,2 & 3 quart saucepans
with lids
(Invest in good ones—
they're not just for melting
bikini wax anymore. . .)*

*Vegetable peeler*

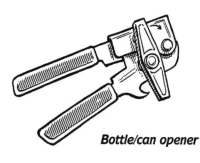

**Bottle/can opener**

*Measuring cups—
wet and dry*

**Vegetable steamer**

*Tongs*

**Medium-sized wire whisk**

**Working corkscrew**

**8″ square glass ovenware
casserole & lid**

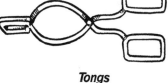

**Colander**

*Set of mixing bowls*

## More Bare Essentials

* 9″ x 13″ baking pan
* 8″ x 8″ baking pan
* 9″ pie pan
* 4″ x 9″ loaf pan
* Baking sheet
* Broiler pan with rack
* Soup ladle
* Cutting board
* Timer
* Heat-proof counter-protector
* Matching salt shaker/pepper mill
* Ice trays
* Teapot
* Matching plates
* Matching knives, forks & spoons

## Versatile Accessories

* Apron (with a clever motto or trendy graphic)
* 2  9″- diameter cake pans
* Double boiler
* Funnel
* Strainer
* Rubber spatula
* Spaghetti rake
* Chopsticks
* Coffeemaker
* Wine caddy
* Cocktail shaker
* Food processor
* Electric mixer
* Blender
* Wok
* Diet scale (for the food, not you. And don't adjust it backward . . .)
* Microwave oven
* Julia Child
* Tom Cruise

# Stock Therapy!

*K*eep these basics on hand and you'll be able to whip up fast repasts that don't taste like last resorts.

## Master Chef Shopping List: *Software*

**Sauces & Oils:** Soy sauce, Worcestershire sauce, canned tomato sauce, tomato paste, chicken broth, beef broth, white vinegar, vegetable oil, olive oil.

**Spices & Seasonings:** Basil, bay leaves, cinnamon, cloves, curry powder, dill weed, garlic*, ginger*, ground/dry mustard, Dijon mustard, nutmeg, oregano, parsley*, black peppercorns*, ground red pepper, white pepper, salt, lemon juice. (If you know people who grow fresh herbs, ask for their surplus.)

**Baking Basics:** All-purpose flour, granulated cane sugar, brown sugar, confectioners' sugar, baking powder, baking soda, cornstarch, vanilla extract, ready-made pie crust, honey.

**Grains:** Pasta, noodles, rice, breadcrumbs.

**Vegetables & Fruit:** Buy fresh whenever possible. Stock potatoes, carrots, onions, lemons, canned whole tomatoes, canned pineapple chunks, frozen vegetables.

**Dairy:** Milk, eggs, butter or margarine.

**Beverages:** Red and white wines, champagne, tea, coffee, bottled water, beer and your favorite liqueurs.

**Plus:** Paper towels, napkins, candles, aluminum foil, plastic wrap, sealable plastic storage bags and sandwich bags, scrubbing pads for non-stick cookware and dish soap.

*Buy fresh for best results.*

# CHAPTER 3

# Turn Your Home Into An Erogenous Zone

## How To Set The Stage For A Dinner To Relish—And A Night To Remember

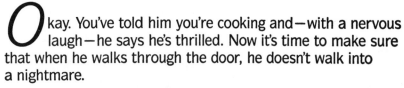

*O*kay. You've told him you're cooking and—with a nervous laugh—he says he's thrilled. Now it's time to make sure that when he walks through the door, he doesn't walk into a nightmare.

Just follow these simple cleaning and preparation tips and you'll make it a memorable evening. . .for all the right reasons.

### The Kitchen . . .

- Cooking aromas whet the appetite, but not if they overpower the senses. Take out the trash. Open windows. Turn on fans. Uncap the air freshener. And give your dog a bath.

- Clean up as you mess up. Don't build a leaning tower of pots and pans in the sink.

- Do you need a roach motel? Or an entire roach convention complex?

- Do you have enough ice cubes? Have they formed into a glacier?

- Did you sweep out all those expired coupons, tattered recipe cards and thousands of used twist ties?

- Did you clean everything from crusty floor to cobwebbed ceiling? Be sure to check the refrigerator top for shriveled black bananas.

**Is this your kitchen?**

## *The Dining & Living Rooms...*

- Did you clear the table and chairs of newspapers, files, spread sheets, status reports, overdue bills, curly faxes . . . ?

- Survey your flatware. Is your set an ensemble of Mom's cast-offs, pilfered pieces and plastic utensils? Or do you have expensive silver that's never made it out of the gift box?

- Program your CD player with soft music that stimulates your appetites.

- Use linen napkins, not folded paper towels, facial tissues or napkins bearing colorful fast-food logos.

- Unclog salt and pepper shakers . . . and wipe away evidence of past meals.

- Grace your table with fresh flowers, scented candles or a bowl of mixed fruit (NOT fruit cocktail). No plastic flowers, waxed fruit or flickering electric candle bulbs.

- Your mother, your slavedriver. For once, listen to her. CLEAN UP THAT MESS. CLOSE THOSE DRAWERS. STAND UP STRAIGHT.

*Is this your "home office?"*

**Don't forget to hide all the toys that need a target.**

# Hints For Single Mothers

- Have a big pizza delivered for your kids, and pick a recipe you're sure will make them turn up their noses.
- Rent 'em all the videos they can watch and promise them a trip to McDonald's the next day if they behave themselves tonight.
- Stash all bicycles, skateboards, basketballs, Big Wheels, bows and arrows, harmonicas, green slime, pet insects, water balloons and bubble-making machines in the locked closet or dog house.
- Secretly remove the batteries from all loud banging toys and boomboxes.
- Slip 'em the latest Nintendo game.
- The easiest method? Pack off the kids to their grandparents or your ex's for the night.

# Hints For Married Women

- Remove those *Dear Abby* clippings from the refrigerator doors—and replace them with a love note addressed to him.
- Don't hand him the shopping list—let him pick up the groceries when *he* does the cooking.
- For once, clear away all your stuff from counters, tabletops, chairs and the sofa.
- No dishwasher? Here's how to get him to help with the dishes: turn to page 97 and select your favorite quick 'n' dirty pick-up line.

## Suggestions For Single Women

- Hide your copies of "How To Be Married One Year From Today," "Smart Women, Stupid Men" and anything by Dr. Ruth. Take down your "Best Buns" calendar.

- Look for press-on nails, lost lingerie, cuff links and other telltale signs of wildlife on dresser tops, under beds and between pillows.

- Isn't it time to stash—or trash—those framed photos of your ex?

- Remove drying undies and pantyhose from the shower curtain rod. Move feminine products out of sight. Empty the trash of telltale wrappers. And hang those stinky running shoes out the window.

- Hide make-up, anti-aging gels and hair coloring. Guys like to think you're naturally gorgeous.

- Get out your list of things that need fixing, like your stereo, TV, VCR, digital clocks, air conditioner, bicycle and car.

*Don't forget to turn off the call monitor on your answering machine.*

# CLAMOUR *Magazine's Dos & Don'ts:*

## *Gals, Watch Out For These Table "Upsettings!"*

**DON'T** get carried away with the centerpiece.
**DO** keep your floral fixations under control.

**DON'T** use chipped or cracked glassware.
**DO** toss them out immediately.

**DON'T** be a Chow-Slinger.
**DO** save those tricks for the rodeo.

**DON'T** clear the table before he's finished eating.
**DO** wait till he swallows his last mouthful.

# *good time guide* #1

## Fill Out Your Mad Licks Dinner Invitation

You are cordially invited for a delicious _____ at home
<br>MEAL

at _____ on _____ to celebrate/honor/enjoy
<br>TIME      DAY      CIRCLE ONE

my _____ . Why don't you bring the fresh _____
<br>NOUN      NOUN

and a dozen _____ just to be safe. For starters, we'll munch
<br>PLURAL NOUN

on buttered _____ and sip ice cold _____ .
<br>PLURAL NOUN      BEVERAGE

I plan to serve baked/roasted/basted/fried/flame-broiled/flambéed/microwaved
<br>CIRCLE ONE

_____ of _____ with _____ sauce and
<br>NOUN      NOUN      NOUN

_____ . For dessert I'm going to vigorously
<br>ONE OR MORE VEGETABLES

_____ some _____ and spread it on your
<br>VERB      NOUN

little _____ . Later, you'll help me wash the _____
<br>NOUN      PLURAL NOUN

in the _____ , which will take until _____ .
<br>ROOM OF HOUSE      TIME OF NEXT MEAL

Then you will give me _____ , buy me
<br>TYPE OF PRECIOUS GEM

_____ and take me on a vacation to _____ .
<br>TYPE OF SPORTS CAR      NAME OF EXOTIC ISLAND

R.S.V.P. _____
<br>PHONE NUMBER

*Now tear this out and fax it to him at his office.*
*And prepare yourself for the _____ of your life.*
<br>VERB

# CHAPTER 4

# The Instant Gourmet Guide To Guys
## A Special Bonus Section for Singles

At first blush, he acts like Mr. Wonderful. But each time he comes over for dinner, he becomes more and more like Mr. Hyde.

Be prepared! This insider's guide is based on the proven theory that a man's table manners closely parallel his bedside manner. Watch for the early warning signs as he reveals his true colors—and the instant you're fed up with him, try the ejection techniques recommended here.

The characters depicted in this section are fictitious. Any resemblance to actual persons living or dead is purely coincidental—and that goes double for you, Ron C. Andrews, Jr. of Pleasantville, Ohio.

29

# AGING JOCK

**Tell-tale signs:** Wears high school letter-jacket—with vents where seams once were. Babbles sports scores. Flexes non-stop. Blows nose in cloth napkins. Guzzles. Drools. Emits belches that register 8.5 on the Richter Scale (secure that china closet!). Fights your dog for bones. Check for opposable thumbs.

**Setting the mood:** Play Springsteen's "Glory Days" and soundtracks from "Rocky I-IV." Load "Sports Bloopers" tape into VCR and watch him come to life.

**Feeding instructions:** Loaves of stale bread, slabs of raw meat, boxes of candy bars. When serving, watch your fingers.

**Suggested drink:** Gatorade by the bucket. Beer by the keg.

**Recommendations:** Spread newspapers. Serve directly from pots. Set beer keg by table, place tube directly in mouth. Reinforce seating. Pack Hefty doggie bag.

**Ejection technique:** Strap trashbag to his belt, throw a football out the door and yell "Hike!"

# TOTAL GEEK

**Tell-tale signs:** Oily hair. Zits. Pocket protector. Pre-stained shirt. Spinach stuck in teeth. Pushes food into little piles. Balls up napkin. Smells food before he eats it. Attracts fruitflies.

**Setting the mood:** Barry Manilow. The Carpenters. "TV Theme Song Sing-Along."

**Feeding instructions:** Chicken dogs, lime Jello, canned mixed vegetables, gummy bears. If he hangs around for breakfast (surely you jest!), Fruit Loops.

**Suggested drink:** Bug juice (with real bugs!).

**Recommendations:** Take your plate and eat in the kitchen.

**Ejection technique:** Explain you have to wash your hair and have to be in bed by 9. As soon as he leaves, invite someone else over.

# MOOCH-O MAN

**Tell-tale signs:** Gets you to pick him up. Doesn't bring anything (except an empty wallet, an empty cooler and a full laundry bag). Asks what's for dinner tomorrow. Bums cab fare home.

**Setting the mood:** Don't. Just hide your CDs, tapes, stereo, Walkman, tools, jewelry, pets, loose change...

**Feeding instructions:** Anything. He'll eat it all, and take home the rest.

**Suggested drink:** Generic cola, preferably flat.

**Recommendations:** Lock liquor cabinet. Padlock fridge. Count silverware before he leaves.

**Ejection technique:** Go to the window and ask him if that's his wallet lying out on the sidewalk. Bolt door and call security.

# TOO-COOL DUDE

**Tell-tale signs:** Dangly earring, gaudy belt buckle, really long hair or really short hair, baggy loud shirts, torn jeans, fringes, instruments, pins and buttons. Carries film canisters (but no camera).

**Setting the mood:** Jazz, Zep, Floyd, Guns 'N' Roses.

**Feeding instructions:** Uncontrolled substances, caffeine, No-Doz.

**Suggested drink:** Jug wine you've previously poured into an empty bottle of Lafite '59.

**Recommendations:** Don't lend him money. And don't bring him home to Mom.

**Ejection technique:** Turn on Top 40 radio station. Ask him when he's going to get a real job, man.

## SENSITIVE VEGGIE

**Tell-tale signs:** Bikes over (Schwinn, not Harley). Socially conscious buttons and T-shirt. No style or fun. Scolds you about everything you eat. Weighs less than you.

**Setting the mood:** Early Dylan, old Baez, "We Are the World," 'Environments' soundtrack (Vol. I-LXVIII).

**Feeding instructions:** Organic veggies. Yogurt dip. Tofu. Trail mix. Carob. No fats or animal by-products or preservatives or food coloring or chemicals or taste.

**Suggested drink:** Skim goat's milk, straight up.

**Recommendations:** Eat dinner before he comes over.

**Ejection technique:** Tell him your "Stuffed Bambi au Jus" just won Blue Ribbon at the NRA Cook-Off.

# *UPPITY YUPPIE*

**Tell-tale signs:** Registered Democrat who votes Republican. Unlisted car phone. BMW with factory fax. Designer condoms. Tells you what to make, how to make it and that he can do it better.

**Setting the mood:** Queasy-listening elevator music.

**Feeding instructions:** Ask his Mum.

**Suggested drink:** Dry martini, shaken, not stirred, brought to him.

**Recommendations:** The operative word is "service." Don't expect him to ever help with anything.

**Ejection technique:** Tell him you just remembered your local NOW chapter meets in 10 minutes. At your place.

# DON JUAN

**Tell-tale signs:** Insatiable appetite, but not for food. Gropes for main dish under table. Keeps dropping his fork. Pants so tight *you* can hardly breathe.

**Setting the mood:** Ravel's Bolero, Prince, Julio Iglesias.

**Feeding instructions:** Raw oysters, chocolate-covered cherries, Vitamin E gel-caps, whipped desserts, soft ice cream (for you) . . .

**Suggested drinks:** Highballs. "Sex-on-the-beach" and Ginseng shooters.

**Recommendations:** Invite your Mom. Dress in layers—maybe 8 or 9. Strap mousetrap to your thigh. Avoid loveseat; sit on end table. Since he's all hands, have him do the dishes.

**Ejection technique:** In your sexiest voice, send him running for passion fruit massage oil. Bolt the door.

# MR. RIGHT

**Tell-tale signs:** Brings the correct wine, expensive chocolates and long-stemmed roses. After dinner, compliments you, does the dishes and asks what you'd like him to cook for you on the next date. Extra credit: related to Donald Trump. Looks like Mel Gibson.

**Setting the mood:** Light the candles, pour the champagne, turn on the charm.

**Feeding instructions:** Anything in this book. Anything he wants.

**Suggested drink:** Dom Perignon.

**Recommendations:** Bolt the door *after* he enters. Plan a full course meal to last, say, a day or two. Study this entire book, then hide it.

**Ejection technique:** Are you kidding!?! Send me his name and phone number!

THE END!

*Chez Moi*
*Menu*

# Enticing Entrees

## Poultry

**Peanut Pasta Chicken**                                  71
Bite-sized chicken tenders smothered in a zesty
peanut sauce served atop a bed of steaming
vermicelli and crisp lettuce.

**Kung Wow Chicken**                                      62
Spicy chicken stir-fry starring crisp snow peas,
fresh mushrooms and red-hot chili peppers in a
savory soy-ginger sauce.

**Ginger Dijon Chicken**                                  73
Boneless chicken breasts pan-fried to perfection
and topped with a mouth-watering ginger-
mustard sauce.

**Good Luck Chicken**                                     76
Juicy chicken breast halves with artichoke
hearts, mushrooms and shallots covered with a
thickened white wine sauce.

**Orange-Glazed Cornish Hens**                            75
Elegant baked game hens stuffed with walnut-
mandarin couscous and brushed with a tangy
orange-Dijon glaze.

**Rock 'n' Roll Chicken***                               113
Layers of prosciutto and mozzarella rolled into
chicken breasts, dipped in Parmesan-bread
crumbs and baked to a juicy finish.

## Vegetarian

**Eggplant Extraordinaire**                               67
Cubes of fresh eggplant in a tangy tomato
sauce topped with freshly grated Parmesan and
served with warm garlic bread.

**Presto Pesto**                                          69
Aromatic fresh basil leaves puréed with butter,
pignolias, garlic and Parmesan cheese and
served on fresh linguine.

**Spicy Three-Cheese Pizza**                              77
Tangy tomato sauce served bubbling hot with
mozzarella, feta and Parmesan cheeses and
your favorite pizza toppings.

**Technicolor Pasta Salad***                             111
Tri-color rotini tossed with seasonal vegetables
and a tangy garlic dressing, served with Hot
Saga Bread.

**Quickie Quiche***                                      117
A cheesy quiche with fresh mushrooms, sautéed
onions and broccoli, seasoned with nutmeg
and baked golden brown.

**Hearty Veggie Medley***                                123
An array of garden-fresh vegetables tossed with
a tangy Dijon vinaigrette dressing.

*\* Serves more than 2*

## Seafood

**Brandy Shrimp**    68
A school of large butterfly shrimp sautéed in garlic butter and artichoke hearts and surrounded with brandy sauce.

**Crab (_His Name Here_)**    66
Delicately broiled crabmeat resplendent with a smooth sauce of melted Swiss cheese, fresh cream and white pepper.

**Crafty Salmon Capers**    63
Thick-cut salmon steaks baked to perfection and drizzled with melted lemon-caper butter.

**Sole Mates**    72
Fresh flounder fillets microwaved in delicious soy-sesame sauce and topped with lightly toasted sesame seeds.

**Chic Thrills Shrimp**    65
Fresh butterfly shrimp swimming in a tangy Dijon-cream sauce and served on a bed of steaming-hot rice.

## Beef & Pasta

**New Wave Lasagna***    112
Zesty layers of beef, cheese and pasta bursting with flavor—cooked entirely in your microwave—noodles and all!

**Stuffed Pasta Perfecto***    119
A premier presentation of jumbo shells stuffed with an enticing blend of cheese, ground beef and tomato sauce.

## Veal & Pork

**Apple Pocket Pork Chops***    118
Juicy pork loins brimming with a succulent apple-raisin filling and coated with a tangy honey-mustard sauce.

**Veal Marsala Magnifique**    64
Tender cutlets and fresh mushrooms sautéed in a delicate garlic-wine sauce.

## Meats

**Flaming Roquefort Steaks**    70
Tempting T-Bones broiled to your liking, oozing with melted roquefort cheese and served flambé at your table.

**Honey Broiled Flank Steak***    74
Tender flank steak marinated in soy, garlic and honey and broiled to the doneness you desire.

**Hot Sausage Superheroes***    127
Hot 'n' spicy Italian sausages simmered in red wine, smothered in peppers, onions and tomatoes and served on hot rolls.

**Superbowlful of Chili***    128
A 3-alarm powerhouse of flavor with ground beef, beans, tomatoes, onions, oregano and cumin—all topped with grated cheddar.

**Jambalaya Jumble***    122
Masterful medley of sausage, ham, chicken and shrimp baked with rice and many spicy delights from The Big Easy.

* Serves more than 2

# Seductive Sideshows

# Sweet Sinsations

# Arouse & Shine

* Serves more than 2

# CHAPTER 6

# The Whine-Free Wine Guide

*Here's How To Find The Perfect Match For Your Meal*

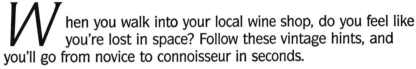

When you walk into your local wine shop, do you feel like you're lost in space? Follow these vintage hints, and you'll go from novice to connoisseur in seconds.

* Expect to pay from $6 to $16 for a good bottle of wine.

* Ask your local wine merchant for recommendations. (If he brings out anything with a screw cap, tell him to go screw it himself.)

* Serve white wine with poultry, fish, veal, lamb, pork.

* Serve red wine with red meat, veal, lamb, pork and salmon.

* Serve blush wine (rosé) on summer days with cold buffets, cookouts and picnics in the park.

* Reserve sweet wine for dessert.

* Match the intensity of the wine to the intensity of the food. The wine should not overpower the entree, and vice versa.

* Serve whites, rosés on champagne chilled (45º-50º). In a pinch, you can quick-chill bottles in your freezer for 30 minutes max.

* Serve most red wines at room temperature (60º-70º). Uncork the bottle at least a half-hour in advance to let it breathe.

* Store wine horizontally. Drink vertically.

* To serve: simply cut away the foil and wipe the top clean. Twist in the corkscrew and pull. For easiest opening method, pass the bottle to your guest.

* If your wine contains natural sediment or cork pieces, pour wine slowly into a broad-mouth decanter, stopping just before the sediment reaches the bottle neck—or strain it through cheesecloth when your guest isn't looking.

* Pour wine into glass and savor the bouquet. Swirl it over your palate, then pour a glass for your guest. Use real wine glasses (no Flintstone jelly jars) and fill them half-way.

CHAPTER 7

# Appetizing Come-Ons

*Set Your Course For Pleasures To Come*

*t*empt your beau with these simple and delicious appetizers and cocktails. It's also a great way to keep him occupied and out of your hair so you can put the finishing touches on dinner.

But go easy. You don't want to make him drowsy—or even worse, fill him up—before the Main Event.

## *Ice Breakers*

### Margarita
Shake with cracked ice: 1 oz. tequila, ½ oz. Triple Sec and 1 oz. lime or lemon juice. Moisten edge of a 3 oz. cocktail glass with cut lime, dip in salt, strain liquid into glass and sip over salty edge.

### Bloody Mary
Shake 1 oz. vodka with 3 oz. tomato juice, 1 Tb. lemon juice, ¼ tsp. horseradish, a dash of Worcestershire sauce, a dash of Tabasco sauce and pepper to taste. Pour over ice into rocks glass and garnish with celery stick or lemon slice.

### Pineapple Daiquiri
Pour over 4 oz. of shaved ice in blender: 2 oz. light rum, 1 tsp. sugar and 2 chunks pineapple. Blend till smooth and pour into cocktail glass.

### White Russian
Pour 1½ oz. vodka and ½ oz. Kahlúa into a rocks glass filled with ice. Stir. Float heavy cream on top.

## Cheery Cherry Tomatoes
### The right stuff.

SERVES 2

6 large cherry tomatoes
⅓ cup low-fat cottage cheese
½ tsp. dill weed
⅛ tsp. garlic powder
1 tsp. lemon juice

**1** Rinse tomatoes, pat dry and pull out stem. Cut in half and gently squeeze out seeds.

**2** In small bowl, mix all other ingredients. Spoon into tomato halves, mounding mixture high. Arrange on a serving plate.

## Baked Brie Meltdown
### It's totally rad!

SERVES 4

8 oz. Brie cheese with rind
1 Tb. butter or margarine, softened to room temperature
2 Tb. almond slivers
Small French bread, thinly sliced
1 apple, rinsed, cored and sliced
8-10 oz. seedless grapes, rinsed

**1** Preheat oven to 350°. Place cheese in a close-fitting ovenware dish. Spread butter on top of cheese and sprinkle with almonds.

**2** Bake uncovered till cheese is hot throughout, 12-14 minutes. Warm the bread in oven 4 minutes before cheese is ready. Serve with fresh fruit.

## Pleasure Platter
### Perfect for the Midnight Munchies, too.

SERVES 2-4

*Select 2 small wedges of the following cheeses:*
Camembert, Gouda, Gruyere, Jarlsberg, Edam or Cheddar
6-8 oz. seedless grapes, rinsed
Your favorite crackers

**1** Unwrap cheeses and cut away any paper and wax. Let cheese come to room temperature.

**2** Place cheese in center of plate and arrange crackers and grapes attractively around cheese. Accompany with a cheese knife and serve.

## Machos
### Hi-octane dip & chips.

SERVES 2

7 oz. bag plain tortilla chips
4 oz. grated Monterey Jack cheese
1 small jar sliced jalapeño peppers
3 green onions (bulb plus 2 inches of green), finely sliced
½ cup sour cream

**1** Pile chips into 8-inch square baking pan and top evenly with grated cheese. Drain liquid from 10-12 sliced jalapeños (or tickle your palate with more) and sprinkle over chips. Turn on broiler.

**2** Slide pan under broiler till cheese-meltdown, 3-4 minutes. Transfer Machos to serving platter with spatula and top with green onions. Accompany with a bowl of sour cream.

## Stuffed Swiss Caps
### The peak of perfection.

SERVES 2

4 large mushrooms
1 tsp. butter or margarine
2 Tb. dried seasoned bread crumbs
2 tsp. Swiss cheese, grated
½ tsp. lemon juice
¼ tsp. parsley flakes
Dashes of salt, pepper and paprika

**1** Wipe mushrooms clean with damp paper towel and pull the stems out of the caps. Finely chop stems and place in small microwave-safe mixing bowl with butter. Zap on High (100%) for 1 minute. Stir in bread crumbs, grated Swiss, lemon juice, parsley, salt and pepper.

**2** Stuff caps with mixture. Place caps stuffed-side-up on serving plate and nuke 2 minutes on High. Sprinkle lightly with paprika and serve.

## Holy Guacamole!
### Heavenly taste—be careful or he'll die for seconds.

SERVES 2-4

2 large ripe avocados
2 green onions (bulb only), minced
½ tsp. ground cumin
3 Tb. lemon juice
2-3 dashes Tabasco hot sauce
Pinch of salt
2-3 large lettuce leaves, rinsed and dried
7 oz. bag fresh tortilla chips
1 tomato, rinsed and cut in wedges

**F.Y.I.**
✱ *Avocado Ripeness Check:* Avocado will yield to pressure from a gentle squeeze.

**1** Cut each avocado in half lengthwise around pit. With a twist, pull avocado halves apart. Slice ¼ inch into pit and twist to remove it.

**2** With a spoon, scoop insides of avocado into a mixing bowl. Add onions, cumin, lemon juice, Tabasco and salt and mash well with fork.

**3** Place lettuce leaves in serving bowl and top with guacamole. Accompany with tortilla chips and tomato slices.

## Fab Crab Dip
### It'll make him keep his claws to himself.

SERVES 4

6 oz. fresh crabmeat, picked clean (or canned, drained)
4 oz. cream cheese, softened to room temperature
2 Tb. onion, minced
1 clove garlic, peeled and minced
½ tsp. curry powder
1 tsp. prepared horseradish
1 Tb. milk
2 tsp. lemon juice

**1** In a large mixing bowl, mash all ingredients together with a fork. Scoop into serving bowl and serve at room temperature. Goes great with bread sticks, crackers and Veg-Out Platter.

## Veg-Out Platter
*The pick of the crop.*

**1** Rinse and slice your favorite fresh vegetables into bite-sized pieces—allow about 8 oz. per person. Arrange attractively on a serving platter, cover and refrigerate till guests arrive. Serve with Fab Crab Dip or your favorite store-bought dip.

***F.Y.I.*** Save time. . .a quick trip to the nearest salad bar makes preparing this appetizer a snap!

## Bowl-Me-Over Spinach Dip
*Strike it rich 'n' creamy.*

SERVES 8

2 cups sour cream
2 large garlic cloves, peeled and minced
4 green onions (bulb plus 2 inches of green), finely chopped
½ red bell pepper, rinsed, seeded and chopped
1 8-oz. frozen spinach, thawed and drained
⅔ cup fresh parsley, finely chopped
2 Tb. Worcestershire sauce
2 dashes Tabasco hot sauce
½ tsp. salt
Big round sourdough bread (or any round, fresh bread loaf)

**1** Place all ingredients except bread in a large mixing bowl. Stir together and chill the dip for 1-2 hours.

**2** Slice top off bread (about ⅛ of the loaf). Pull bread from hollow and tear into bite-sized pieces.

**3** At party time, fill bread shell with dip and serve with bread chunks on the side.

## Ham-It-Up Melon
*"Honey dew this, honey dew that. . . ."*

SERVES 2-4

½ ripe honeydew melon, chilled
6 oz. paper-thin slices of prosciutto ham, chilled
Freshly ground black pepper

**1** Cut melon in half, scoop out seeds and cut away rind. Slice melon into thin crescents and cut prosciutto to size of crescents.

**2** Place alternate slices of ham and melon on serving plates, sprinkle lightly with pepper and serve.

## Bewitching Cocktails

Here's how to pass your bar exam: just mix up these provocative potions before dinner. Bon Aperitif!

### (*Your State Here*) Cooler

Into a tall glass, mix ½ glass white wine, ¼ glass orange juice and ¼ glass 7-Up. Garnish with lemon and lime wedges.

### Zesty Sangria

Into a tall glass, mix ½ glass red wine and ⅓ glass cranberry juice. Top with a splash *each* of brandy and 7-Up. Garnish with orange slices.

### Fuzzy Navel

Into a tall glass, mix 2 parts peach schnapps with 1 part vodka and 3 parts orange juice.

### Cape Codder

Into a tall glass filled with ice, add 1 oz. vodka and fill glass with cranberry juice.

### Screwdriver

Into a tall glass filled with ice, add 1 oz. vodka and fill glass with fresh-squeezed orange juice.

**Mocktails**—No alcohol. No hangover. No sin.

### Yuppie Tamer

Into a rocks glass filled with ice, mix ½ glass cranberry juice with ½ glass club soda. Garnish with an orange slice.

### Bobbin' Robin

Mix ⅔ glass orange juice with ⅓ glass 7-Up plus ½ oz. grenadine and shake. Garnish with orange wedges or Maraschino cherries.

### Virgin Sunrise

Into a rocks glass filled with ice, pour fresh-squeezed orange juice. Top with a few drops of grenadine.

CHAPTER 8

# Sensuous Salads

### Iceberg Is Only The Tip

Once your guests surrender to these temptations of the fresh, ordinary salad bar fare will wilt in comparison.

## Hints To Make The World's Greatest Salad

Many grocery stores now offer you the convenience of a salad bar, saving you the rinsing and cutting and deciding what to do with ⅔ of a head of leftover lettuce. If there's no salad bar in your area, here are a few hints to help you make a great salad:

✱ Rinse everything thoroughly under cold water—especially spinach—and shake or pat dry with paper towels. But don't rinse greens before you refrigerate them unless you're going to use them the same day.

✱ Buy only fresh, ripe vegetables and fruit. Avoid yellow, wilted or dry outer lettuce leaves. To remove the leaves from a head of lettuce, rap the solid core against the kitchen counter and pry off the core. Hold the head upside down under cold running water to rinse.

✱ Tear salad greens by hand into pieces instead of cutting them with a knife.

✱ Add just enough dressing to coat the salad lightly—don't overpower the fresh taste of the vegetables. And be sure to add the dressing right before serving.

# Bravocado Salad
*They'll hunger for an encore.*

SERVES 2-3

## PrepTime
10 minutes

## Pantry Raid
Paper towels, vegetable peeler, serrated knife, salad bowls

## Grocery Guide
⅓ head of red leaf lettuce or any leafy lettuce, rinsed and patted dry
1 medium-sized ripe avocado
1 grapefruit, peeled and sectioned into bite-sized pieces
½ red onion, thinly sliced
salt and freshly ground pepper

*For The Dressing:*
Your favorite vinaigrette or sweet dressing

**1** Cut avocado in half lengthwise around pit. With a twist, pull avocado halves apart. Slice ¼ inch into pit and twist to remove it. Peel the skin and cut into lengthwise slices.

**2** Check the grapefruit sections to make sure you've removed all the bitter white pith, and set 4 sections aside.

**3** Line salad bowls with lettuce. Place alternate slices of avocado and grapefruit in "spoke" pattern on top of lettuce. Sprinkle with onion rings and season lightly with salt and pepper. Drizzle with dressing, and squeeze juice from remaining 4 grapefruit sections equally over salads. Serve!

### F.Y.I.
✱ *Avocado Ripeness Check:* Avocado will yield to pressure from a gentle squeeze.
✱ For a change of taste, substitute 2 navel oranges for the grapefruit.

# TCBS* Salad
**\*The Country's Best Salad**

SERVES 2

**1** On salad plates, place tomato slices in a single layer. Top with slices of mozzarella cheese.

**2** In a small bowl, mix olive oil and vinegar. Drizzle over mozzarella, then sprinkle with basil and season lightly with pepper. Serve at room temperature.

### F.Y.I.
✱ For visual variety, alternate pairs of cheese/tomato with the tomato on top.
✱ Or, cut the mozzarella into cubes and the tomatoes into wedges and continue at Step 2.

## PrepTime
5 minutes

## Pantry Raid
Salad plates, small mixing bowl, serrated knife

## Grocery Guide
1 large fresh tomato, thinly sliced
2-4 oz. fresh mozzarella cheese, thinly sliced
1 Tb. olive oil
1 tsp. red wine vinegar
2 Tb. fresh basil, chopped
Freshly ground black pepper

# Marvelous Mandarin Salad
*It looks (and tastes) mah-velous. . . .*

**PrepTime**
7 minutes

**Pantry Raid**
Large salad bowl, small mixing bowl, paper towels

**Grocery Guide**
8 romaine lettuce leaves, rinsed, patted dry and torn into bite-sized pieces
1 11-oz. can mandarin orange segments, drained and juice reserved
½ cup pecan pieces
½ cup herbed croutons (optional)

**1** Place lettuce in a large salad bowl and top with mandarin oranges and pecan pieces.

**2** *For the dressing:* Add 3 Tb. reserved mandarin orange juice into small bowl. Mix in mustard, olive oil, salt and pepper. Mix well. Pour over salad and toss to coat. Add croutons, if desired.

*For The Dressing:*
2 tsp. Dijon mustard
2 Tb. olive oil
¼ tsp. salt
½ tsp. freshly ground black or white pepper

# Cherry Hearts Salad
*It's a real heartthrob.*

SERVES 2

**1** Line salad bowls with lettuce leaves.

**2** Top lettuce with equal amounts of tomato halves and hearts of palm (and onion rings if you're serving Certs for dessert).

**3** In mixing bowl, whisk basil, vinegar and olive oil. Season lightly with salt and white pepper to your liking. Drizzle over salad and serve.

*For The Dressing:*
2 Tb. finely chopped fresh basil (or 1 Tb. dried basil)
2 Tb. Balsamic or other white vinegar
2 Tb. olive oil
Salt and white pepper

**PrepTime**
10 minutes

**Pantry Raid**
Two salad bowls, small mixing bowl, whisk or fork

**Grocery Guide**
2 large lettuce leaves, rinsed and patted dry
½ lb. cherry tomatoes, rinsed, stems removed and cut in half
1 8-oz. can hearts of palm, drained thoroughly, rinsed and cut into ½-inch slices
¼ Bermuda onion, sliced thinly into rings (optional)

# Cool-As-A-Cucumber Salad
## Chop up and chill out!

**PrepTime**
5 minutes

**Pantry Raid**
Small mixing bowl

**Grocery Guide**
1 medium-sized cucumber, peeled
   and cut into ¼-inch coins
2 fresh ripe tomatoes, rinsed and
   cut into wedges
½ medium-sized Bermuda onion,
   sliced

*For The Dressing:*
Basil Vinaigrette from Cherry
   Hearts Salad

**1** Combine cucumber, tomatoes and onion in individual salad bowls.

**2** Drizzle with dressing, toss and serve.

**F.Y.I.**
* As a side dish for the Salmon Capers, substitute dill for the basil in the dressing.

---

# Strong-To-The-Finish Spinach Salad
## Popeye's favorite with no olive oil.

SERVES 2

**1** Rinse spinach leaves thoroughly under running water and pat dry with paper towels. Pull off stems and discard.

**2** Add spinach to salad bowls and toss with onions, mushrooms, tomato, dressing, salt and pepper. Serve!

**PrepTime**
10 minutes

**Pantry Raid**
Paper towels, 2 salad bowls

**Grocery Guide**
6 oz. fresh spinach
¼ red onion, peeled and thinly
   sliced
8 fresh mushrooms, wiped clean
   and thinly sliced
1 medium-sized tomato, cut into
   wedges
¼ tsp. salt
½ tsp. freshly ground pepper

*For The Dressing:*
Your favorite poppy seed dressing
   or mustard vinaigrette

# Seize 'Em Salad
*Et tu, Crouton.*

**PrepTime**
20 minutes

**Pantry Raid**
Large salad bowl, medium-sized saucepan with cover, large spoon, whisk or fork

**Grocery Guide**
1 large garlic clove, peeled and halved
½ tsp. dry powdered mustard
½ tsp. freshly ground black pepper
¼ tsp. salt
1 tsp. Worcestershire sauce
¼ cup olive oil
1 head romaine lettuce, rinsed and torn into small pieces
1 egg
1½ Tb. lemon juice
1½ cups Crouton Call croutons or store bought
¼ cup grated Parmesan cheese

*Optional:* 4 anchovy fillets, drained and minced

**1** Rub inside of salad bowl with cut surfaces of garlic. Then mince garlic and add to bowl. Into garlic, mix mustard, pepper, salt and Worcestershire sauce. Whisk in olive oil, add lettuce pieces and toss well.

**2** Boil enough water in saucepan to cover the egg. Gently place egg (do not crack shell) in boiling water for 10 seconds, then remove pan from heat, cover, and let stand 30 seconds. With large spoon, remove egg to cold running water till cool.

**3** Break egg into center of salad, pour lemon juice directly on egg and toss well to coat the lettuce. Refrigerate up to 30 minutes, if desired.

**4** When ready to serve, add croutons, Parmesan cheese and anchovies and toss well.

# Crouton Call

**1** Preheat oven to 400°. Trim crusts from bread. Butter both sides and cut into ½-inch cubes.

**2** Transfer to ungreased baking sheet, sprinkle lightly with garlic powder and basil and bake, uncovered, 10 minutes; turn croutons and bake until crisp and golden, about 10 minutes more. Add to salad right before serving.

**Grocery Guide**
2 slices day-old or stale bread
Butter or margarine
⅛ tsp. garlic powder
Dash of dried basil

55

# CHAPTER 9

# Steamy Soups

*Stir In Passion
By The Bowlful*

Nothing warms the soul like a bowl of hearty homemade soup. (But beware: you can guarantee he'll rely on you every time he comes down with a cold.)

### Hints To Make The World's Best Soup

✳ Don't let your garnish be garish. Try one of these simple garnishes to class up your soup: chopped parsley or tiny whole parsley sprigs, chopped green onions, croutons, grated Parmesan, thin strips of carrot, lemon or orange slices or fresh herbs.

✳ Sample before serving. Make sure you taste-test your soup right before it's time to serve—the taste of some soup ingredients has a habit of becoming absorbed by other ingredients and disappearing. Adjust the seasonings by adding a dash more herbs just before serving.

✳ Too busy to prepare soup? Buy a can of your favorite premium soup and toss the can. Garnish soup with a dash of sherry and herbed croutons. If he compliments your soup, say "thank you" and change the subject to sports.

✳ And above all, don't slurp!

# Easy Egg Drop Soup
*Drop everything—soup's on!*

**PrepTime**
5 minutes

**CookTime**
5 minutes

**Pantry Raid**
Large saucepan, ladle

**Grocery Guide**
2 cups chicken broth (from can or
  bouillon cube)
1 green onion (bulb plus 2 inches
  of green), minced
¼ tsp. sugar
½ tsp. soy sauce
1 Tb. cornstarch
1 egg, lightly beaten with 1 Tb.
  cold water
Crispy Chinese noodles (optional)

**1** Heat chicken broth in saucepan over medium heat. Add green onion and bring to boil.

**2** In small cup, blend cornstarch with 2 Tb. water.

**3** Into broth, stir sugar, soy sauce and cornstarch mixture till slightly thickened. Bring to full boil, remove from heat and drizzle in half the egg mixture, stirring gently to cook and separate egg. Ladle into soup bowls, top with crispy noodles and enjoy!

# Clamor-For-More Clam Chowder
*A pre-dinner simmer.*

SERVES 3-4

**1** In saucepan, melt butter at medium heat. Add onions and sauté 6 minutes, or till onions are light golden.

**2** Open cans of clams and drain only the liquid into saucepan. Add potatoes, salt and Old Bay. Cover and simmer 10 minutes or till potatoes are nearly tender, stirring occasionally.

**3** Add clams and half & half, cover and reduce heat to low. Simmer 5 minutes or till heated through. Stir. Ladle into soup bowls and sprinkle lightly with paprika. Serve with oyster crackers.

**F.Y.I.**
✳ If Old Bay is not available in your area, substitute ⅛ tsp. celery seed, ¼ tsp. dry mustard and ¼ tsp. ground red pepper.

**PrepTime**
8 minutes

**CookTime**
25 minutes

**Pantry Raid**
Large saucepan with cover

**Grocery Guide**
1 small onion, peeled and minced
1 Tb. butter or margarine
2 (6½-oz.) cans chopped clams,
  juice reserved
½ lb. potatoes, peeled and cut
  into ½-inch cubes
⅛ tsp. salt.
1 tsp. Old Bay seasoning
1 cup half & half
⅛ tsp. paprika

# Mmm-Mmm-Better Vegetable Soup
*Everything but the kitchen sink.*

### PrepTime
15 minutes

### CookTime
45 minutes

### Pantry Raid
Large pot with cover, grater, ladle

### Grocery Guide
3 Tb. butter or margarine
2 small potatoes, peeled and cut into ½-inch cubes
1 small yellow onion, peeled and sliced
2 cups shredded green cabbage
2 carrots, peeled and sliced into ¼-inch coins
1 small zucchini or yellow squash, rinsed, ends trimmed, sliced into ¼-inch coins
½ cup shelled or frozen peas
8 oz. can tomato sauce
1 chicken bouillon cube
1 tsp. dried basil
2 cloves garlic, peeled and minced
Salt and freshly ground black pepper

**1** In pot, melt butter over medium heat. Add potatoes, onion, cabbage, carrots, zucchini and peas and cook 4 minutes, stirring occasionally.

**2** Stir in tomato sauce, 1½ cups water, bouillon cube, basil and garlic. Season lightly with salt and pepper.

**3** Cover, reduce heat to low and simmer for 45 minutes, stirring occasionally. Adjust seasonings to your liking and serve.

### F.Y.I.
✳ For a change of taste, mound 1 tsp. grated Parmesan cheese in center of each bowl of hot soup.
✳ Serve soup hot, or make ahead and serve chilled. Soup refrigerates and freezes well.

# Almost Grandma's Chicken Soup
*For the chief executive who wants to be executive chef.*

SERVES 3-4

### PrepTime
5 minutes

### CookTime
15 minutes

### Pantry Raid
Large pot, vegetable peeler, ladle

### Grocery Guide
1 cup skinned, boned and diced chicken meat
1 cup uncooked egg noodles
4 chicken bouillon cubes
1 carrot, peeled into strips
¼ tsp. freshly ground black pepper
2 tsp. minced parsley (or 1 tsp. dried parsley)

**1** In large pot, bring 1 quart of water to boil at high heat. Reduce heat to medium, add chicken pieces and cook for 2 minutes.

**2** Stir in noodles, bouillon cubes and carrot strips. Season with pepper and simmer uncovered till noodles are cooked al dente, about 7 minutes. Stir occasionally.

**3** Mix in parsley and additional pepper, if desired, and serve hot!

CHAPTER 10

# Enticing Entrees

*Kiss KPA Goodbye With*
*These Main Attractions*

C an you say *"Purée de Crevettes a l'Étouffe de Barnacles au Beurre?"* How about *"Crème de Boeuf Ecrasé sur le Capot de Citroën?"* Qu'est-ce que c'est wha-a-at?! If these dishes are this hard to pronounce, just imagine what it's like to prepare them. Impossible cooking times. Exotic (and possibly extinct) ingredients. All four burners going at once. And a 60-step sequence just for the sauce.

No wonder today's busy career woman is reluctant—no, intimidated—no, downright paralyzed—to set foot in the kitchen!

That's why you'll find these easy-to-follow recipes will help you wow your audience without wearing you out.

## good time guide #2:
### Secrets To Producing A Four-Star Presentation

**Before cooking:** Read your recipe carefully before starting. Create a backwards timetable so all dishes finish together. Assemble your ingredients. Thaw frozen items, if necessary. Pre-slice and pre-chop as indicated. Let refrigerated foods come to room temperature. And review the tips and secrets in the back of this book.

**During cooking:** Keep an eye on the clock. Work quickly, stay calm. Pour something to drink. Set the table. Dim the lights. Ignite the candles and relax!

**Before serving:** Arrange food attractively on each plate and serve hot. Garnish with color and zest: a sprig of fresh parsley or watercress. . . .a wedge of lemon or orange  . . carrot strips or green onion tops.

# $\mathscr{K}$ung Wow Chicken
## *You'll wok their socks off!*

---

**PrepTime**
20 minutes

**CookTime**
10 minutes

**Pantry Raid**
Wok or large frying pan, medium-sized mixing bowl, medium-sized saucepan with cover, spatula

**Grocery Guide**
½ cup uncooked long grain or converted white rice
¾ lb. boneless, skinless chicken breasts, cut into 1-inch cubes
3-4 dried small red chili peppers, whole
3 Tb. vegetable oil
½ cup shelled peanuts or cashews
14 snow peas, stems removed
8-10 medium-sized mushrooms, wiped clean and thinly sliced
3 green onions (bulb plus 2 inches of green), thinly sliced
2 garlic cloves, peeled and minced
1 tsp. sesame oil

*For the sauce:*
1 Tb. cornstarch
¼ cup chicken broth (from bouillon cube or can)
1½ Tb. soy sauce
1½ Tb. dry sherry or rice wine
¼ tsp. ground ginger
1 tsp. sugar

---

**Platemates**
Easy Egg Drop Soup (page 58)

**No-Whine Wine Guide**
California Gewürztraminer or dry Chenin Blanc

**1** Start rice according to directions on package. Begin Step 3 five minutes before rice is ready.

**2** *Prepare the sauce:* In mixing bowl, stir together 1 Tb. cornstarch with 1 Tb. chicken broth. Stir in remaining broth, soy sauce, sherry, ginger and sugar and set aside.

**3** In wok, heat 2 Tb. vegetable oil on high heat. When oil is rippling hot, carefully add whole chili peppers and stir-fry them till they turn black. (You may take 'em out or leave 'em in for extra heat.)

**4** Add chicken cubes and peanuts and stir-fry 2 minutes only. Transfer everything from wok onto clean plate.

**5** Lower heat to medium, add remaining 1 Tb. vegetable oil and stir-fry snow peas, mushrooms, green onions and garlic for 1 minute.

**6** Return chicken mixture to wok, increase heat, and stir-fry 1 minute more. Pour in sauce and stir-fry until sauce thickens slightly (about 1 minute—don't overcook!). Remove wok from heat and mix in 1 tsp. sesame oil. Serve immediately over hot rice.

---

**F.Y.I.**
✳ Chili peppers are 3-Alarmers: warn your guests not to chew them.

✳ Impress your guest with chopsticks—unless he'll need to teach you how to use them . . .

# Crafty Salmon Capers
## He'll swim upstream for these baked beauties.

4 minutes
**CookTime**
20-25 minutes
**Pantry Raid**
Baking pan or dish (approx.
8"-square), small mixing bowl,
spatula, paper towels
**Grocery Guide**
2 fresh salmon steaks, about
¾-inch thick and 6 oz. each
2 Tb. butter, softened to room
temperature
2 tsp. capers
1 tsp. lemon juice (cut lemon
slices for garnish)
Freshly ground black pepper

**Platemates**
Cool-As-A-Cucumber Salad (page
54) or TCBS Salad (page 52)
with toasted French bread
**F.Y.I.**
✱ *Salmon Doneness Check*: Serve
when flesh is a paler pink all
the way through and slightly
springy, not spongy and not
hard.
✱ For a spicy kick, add a pinch of
red cayenne pepper to the
caper butter.
**No-Whine Wine Guide**
California Sauvignon Blanc (a/k/a
Fumé Blanc)

**1** Grease bottom of baking dish with 1 Tb. butter. Then preheat oven to 350º.

**2** Place salmon in dish in single layer and bake uncovered for 20-25 minutes or till done (see Doneness Check).

**3** Meanwhile, rinse and pat the capers dry with paper towels.

**4** In mixing bowl, smooosh capers with back of soup spoon. Mash together with remaining 1 Tb. softened butter and lemon juice and season lightly with pepper.

**5** When salmon are ready (don't overcook!), transfer to dinner plates. Immediately top evenly with lemon-caper butter and fresh lemon slices. Serve hot!

# Veal Marsala Magnifique
## Bravo! Bravissimo! Awesome!

SERVES 2

**PrepTime**
10 minutes

**CookTime**
10 minutes

**Pantry Raid**
10"-12" non-stick frying pan,
slotted spoon, small mixing bowl,
flat mallet or small saucepan,
aluminum foil, non-metal spatula,
plastic wrap or wax paper

**Grocery Guide**
¾ lb. boneless veal cutlets, cut
  ⅓-inch thick
¼ cup all-purpose flour
⅛ tsp. freshly ground black
  pepper
4 Tb. butter or margarine
4 medium-sized mushrooms,
  wiped clean and thinly sliced
¼ cup Marsala wine
1 garlic clove, peeled and crushed
1 lemon, cut into wedges
Fresh parsley sprigs

**Platemates**
Confetti Rice (page 80)

**F.Y.I.**
✱ If your frying pan is too small
  to hold all the cutlets in a
  single layer, cook in two
  batches.
✱ For a change of taste,
  substitute ¾ pound boneless,
  skinless chicken breasts for the
  veal.

**1** Place one cutlet between 2 sheets of plastic wrap. With flat mallet or bottom of a small saucepan, gently pound cutlet till it's about ¼-inch flat. Repeat for each cutlet.

**2** Add flour onto clean plate and mix in pepper. Dip cutlets into flour to coat all sides evenly. Set aside.

**3** In frying pan, melt 2 Tb. butter on medium heat, tilting pan to coat bottom. Add mushrooms and sauté 3 minutes. Transfer to bowl.

**4** Return frying pan to medium heat and melt remaining 2 Tb. butter, tilting pan to coat bottom. When butter sizzles, add veal in single layer and fry till lightly browned, about 2 minutes. Flip and fry till lightly browned again, about 2 minutes more. Transfer cutlets to serving plates and cover with aluminum foil to keep warm.

**5** On medium heat, stir wine and garlic into frying pan and bring to boil. Scrape pan with non-metal spatula to loosen browned pieces from bottom. Add mushrooms and stir 1 minute more. Pour mixture over veal, garnish with lemon wedges and parsley sprigs and serve.

**No-Whine Wine Guide**
Beaujolais or Merlot

# Chic Thrills Shrimp
## Enticing treats from the deep.

**PrepTime**
20 minutes

**CookTime**
6 minutes

**Pantry Raid**
Large frying pan, spatula

**Grocery Guide**
½ cup uncooked long grain or
   converted white rice
2 Tb. butter
¾ lb. medium-sized raw shrimp,
   shelled and deveined
3 Tb. chopped shallots
½ tsp. paprika
½ tsp. red cayenne pepper
⅛ tsp. freshly ground black
   pepper
Dash salt
2 Tb. Dijon mustard
¼ cup heavy cream
¼ cup sour cream or plain (not
   vanilla) yogurt
1 Tb. dried parsley flakes

**F.Y.I.**
* This is a rapid-fire recipe. Make
  sure all your ingredients are
  lined-up and ready for the
  exciting finale.
* *Shrimp Doneness Check:*
  Shrimp cook quickly—they're
  ready when their color changes
  from white to pink throughout.
* If rice is ready before shrimp,
  remove from heat and keep
  covered.

**1** Cook rice according to directions on package. Begin Step 2 five minutes before rice is ready.

**2** In frying pan, melt butter on medium heat, tilting pan to coat bottom. Add shallots and sauté till soft, 2-3 minutes.

**3** Add shrimp, paprika, red pepper, black pepper and salt and sauté 2 minutes more.

**4** Stir in mustard and heavy cream. Simmer till thickened, 2-3 minutes and remove pan from heat.

**5** Stir in sour cream and parsley. Return pan to low heat and warm sauce throughout *but don't let it boil*.

**6** Spoon rice onto dinner plates and top equally with shrimp and sauce. Garnish with sprigs of parsley.

**No-Whine Wine Guide**
Dry Bordeaux (Graves or Mouton-
   Cadet) or Sauvignon Blanc

**Platemates**
Cherry Hearts Salad (page 53)

# Crab (His Name Here)
## Guaranteed to turn your crab into a king.

### PrepTime
10 minutes

### CookTime
10 minutes

### Pantry Raid
Small saucepan, 2 ovenproof serving dishes or an 8-inch square glass ovenware dish, large serving spoon

### Grocery Guide
8 oz. crabmeat (if frozen, allow time to thaw)
2 Tb. butter or margarine
1 Tb. all-purpose flour
½ cup whole milk
2 Tb. whipping cream
¼ cup Swiss cheese, grated
½ tsp. ground white pepper
½ tsp. Worcestershire sauce
4-8 dashes Tabasco hot sauce
1 tsp. lemon juice (cut lemon into wedges for garnish)

### Platemates
Strong-To-The-Finish Spinach Salad (page 54)

### F.Y.I.
* Pick through the crabmeat and pull out all the shells the professional pickers missed.
* Score extra points by serving this dish in scallop-shaped shells or ramekins.

**1** Add crabmeat to ovenware dish—or divide evenly between two ovenproof serving dishes. Then set broiler rack 5 inches from heat source.

**2** In small saucepan on low heat, melt 2 Tb. butter—don't let it burn! Pour *half* the melted butter onto crabmeat and mix.

**3** Return saucepan to burner on low heat and stir flour into remaining butter till smooth. Pour in milk and whipping cream and stir constantly until sauce thickens and bubbles. Set oven to broil now.

**4** Remove saucepan from heat and immediately stir in grated cheese, white pepper, Worcestershire sauce, Tabasco and lemon juice. Return to low heat and stir till smooth and bubbly again.

**5** Pour hot mixture over crabmeat—do not stir. Broil 3 minutes or till top is bubbly and lightly browned. If single ovenware dish was used, spoon crab into individual serving dishes. Garnish with lemon wedges and serve immediately.

### No-Whine Wine Guide
Dry Graves, White Bordeaux or
  Dry Riesling

# Eggplant Extraordinaire
## Egg 'em on with this meatless wonder.

### PrepTime
10 minutes

### CookTime
10 minutes

### Pantry Raid
2 quart microwave-safe casserole dish with cover, large serving spoon, microwave-safe serving plate

### Grocery Guide
1 firm medium-sized eggplant, about 1¼ lb.
16 oz. zesty spaghetti sauce
3 Tb. butter or margarine, softened to room temperature
1 medium-sized yellow onion, finely chopped
1 green bell pepper, seeded, rinsed and chopped
2 garlic cloves, peeled and chopped
½ tsp. oregano
½ tsp. salt
⅛ tsp. freshly ground black pepper
1 Tb. grated Parmesan cheese

### Platemates
TCBS Salad (page 52), Golden Garlic Bread (page 84)

### F.Y.I.
∗ Accompany with a small bowl of freshly grated Parmesan cheese.

### No-Whine Wine Guide
Valpolicella or Bardolino

**1** Rinse eggplant and cut in half lengthwise. Cut around the inside ¼ inch from edge and carefully scoop out interior without breaking skin.

**2** Cut eggplant interior into small cubes and add to casserole dish. Stir in spaghetti sauce, butter, onion, green pepper, garlic, oregano, salt and pepper. Mix thoroughly.

**3** Cover casserole and microwave on High (100%) for 2 minutes. Stir. Cover and microwave 2 more minutes and stir again.

**4** Spoon mixture into eggplant shells and top with grated Parmesan cheese. Place filled shells on serving plate and microwave on High, uncovered, 5-6 minutes or until eggplant is tender. Let stand 5 minutes and serve.

# *B*randy Shrimp With Artichoke Hearts
## *Savor these affairs of the heart.*

SERVES 2

---

**PrepTime**
25 minutes

**CookTime**
8 minutes

**Pantry Raid**
Large frying pan, slotted spatula or spoon, paper towels

**Grocery Guide**
½ cup uncooked long grain or converted white rice
4 unmarinated canned artichoke hearts
4 Tb. butter
2 garlic cloves, peeled and minced
¾ lb. medium-sized raw shrimp, shelled and deveined
6 mushrooms, wiped clean and thinly sliced
1 tomato, seeded and chopped
¼ cup brandy
½ tsp. lemon juice
Salt and freshly ground black pepper

**F.Y.I.**
* This is a rapid-fire recipe. Make sure all your ingredients are lined-up and ready for the exciting finale.
* *Shrimp Doneness Check:* Shrimp cook quickly—they're ready when their color changes from white to pink throughout.
* To easily seed the tomato, cut in half crosswise and gently squeeze each half to remove seeds.

**1** Start rice according to directions on package. Begin Step 3 five minutes before rice is ready.

**2** Remove excess liquid from artichoke hearts by gently pressing with paper towels. Cut artichokes into quarters and set aside. Cut 2 Tb. butter into tiny pieces and chill in refrigerator.

**3** In frying pan on medium heat, melt the remaining 2 Tb. butter, tilting pan to coat bottom. Add garlic and sauté 10 seconds. Add shrimp, sautéing and flipping until all shrimp turn pink, 3 minutes max. With slotted spoon, remove shrimp and set aside.

**4** Add mushrooms and tomatoes to frying pan and sauté 3 minutes on medium heat.

**5** Add quartered artichoke hearts and shrimp and sauté 1 minute more. Pour in ¼ cup brandy and ½ tsp. lemon juice and stir together for 10 seconds. Remove pan from heat. Don't overcook!

**6** Immediately dot with pieces of butter from refrigerator and stir to melt. Season lightly with salt and pepper and serve immediately over hot rice.

---

**No-Whine Wine Guide**
California Sauvignon Blanc (a/k/a Fumé Blanc)

**Platemates**
Boogie Woogie Broccoli (page 84)

# Presto Pesto
## *As romantic as dinner in Venice. Well . . . almost.*

**PrepTime**
15 minutes

**CookTime**
10 minutes

**Pantry Raid**
Large pot, food processor

**Grocery Guide**
1 cup (½ oz.) fresh basil leaves,
  picked from stem
¼ cup olive oil
1½ Tb. butter, softened to room
  temperature
1 Tb. pine nuts (pignolias)
2 garlic cloves, peeled
⅛ tsp. salt
¼ cup grated Parmesan cheese
8 oz. linguine
Freshly ground black pepper

**Platemates**
TCBS Salad (page 52), Golden
  Garlic Bread (page 84)

**F.Y.I.**
* If you don't own a food
  processor, a blender will do
  just fine.
* Don't even think about using
  dried basil for this dish!
* Accompany with a small bowl
  of grated Parmesan cheese as
  a garnish.

**No-Whine Wine Guide**
Pinot Grigio

**1** In large pot, bring 3 quarts of water to a rapid boil.

**2** Meanwhile, in a food processor, purée basil leaves, olive oil, butter, pine nuts, garlic and salt until ingredients are nearly smooth. Stir in the Parmesan cheese.

**3** Put linguine in boiling water and follow package directions for al dente cooking time. Stir occasionally.

**4** Drain linguine. Return linguine to pot and toss with pesto sauce. Season lightly with freshly ground pepper to your liking. Serve the pesto at room temperature!

# *Flaming Roquefort Steaks*
## *Serve him the steak and the sizzle!*

*PrepTime*     *CookTime*
7 minutes     12 minutes

### Pantry Raid
Aluminum foil, medium-sized mixing bowl, tongs, small saucepan (or small microwave-safe bowl), oven mitt

### Grocery Guide
2 T-bone or sirloin steaks, 1½-inches thick, about ¾ lb. each
3 Tb. Roquefort or blue cheese, crumbled
2 Tb. butter, softened to room temperature
2 Tb. brandy
Freshly ground black pepper

### Platemates
Magic Skillet Mushrooms (page 80), Top 40 Potatoes (page 85)

### F.Y.I.
* Don't over-broil topping or you'll turn your blue cheese to brown!
* Don't be intimidated if this is your first flaming entree. But in the event of a runaway flambé, don't panic. Flames will quickly die down, especially if you cover them with a frying pan lid.

### No-Whine Wine Guide
Chateauneuf-du-Pape or Petite Sirah

**1** Line broiler pan with aluminum foil to save messy clean-up. Set oven rack to level where top of meat will be 3 inches from heat source. Preheat broiler 5 minutes. Meanwhile, slash through fat along edge of steak (not into meat) at 1-inch intervals to prevent curling.

**2** Place steaks on pan with fat edge of steaks towards back (to reduce spattering) and broil about 6 minutes (less if steak is thinner than 1½ inches). Meanwhile, in mixing bowl, mash together Roquefort and butter with fork.

**3** Flip steaks with tongs and broil second side about 5½ minutes for medium-rare, or until it's *nearly* cooked to your liking when slashed at the thickest portion.

**4** Meanwhile, warm brandy in small saucepan over low heat, or microwave in small microwave-safe bowl for 30 seconds on High (100%).

**5** With oven mitt, pull out broiler pan half-way. Smear cheese mixture on top of steaks. Slide pan back under broiler for 30 seconds only.

**6** Transfer steaks to serving plates and season lightly with freshly ground pepper. Dim house lights. At table, carefully ignite warm brandy and pour the blue-flaming liquid over steaks. *Voila!*

# Peanut Pasta Chicken
## A tempting hot peanut sauce. (Say it three times fast.)

SERVES 2

**1** In a large pot, heat 3 quarts of water to simmer (just below boil). Add chicken pieces and simmer 5 minutes (or till chicken is no longer pink throughout). Remove chicken with slotted spoon and set aside on clean plate.

**2** Increase heat and bring water to full boil. Add vermicelli and follow package directions for al dente cooking time. Drain in colander.

**3** *Prepare the sauce:* While vermicelli cooks, into bowl thoroughly mix peanut butter, sugar, ground red pepper, vinegar, soy sauce, oil and garlic with 2 Tb. water.

**4** Into peanut sauce, stir the cooked chicken with red bell pepper and zucchini slivers.

**5** On each dinner plate, arrange a single portion of noodles in a circle. Place shredded lettuce in center and top with chicken-peanut mixture. Sprinkle with chopped peanuts and serve!

**F.Y.I.**
* If you're serving fresh vermicelli with a shorter cooking time, save Step 2 till *after* Step 4.

* If a warmer sauce is desired, at Step 5, microwave the mixture 2 minutes on High (100%) before placing on lettuce bed.

# Sole Mates
## Zesty fillets for your heart 'n' soul.

**PrepTime**
7 minutes

**CookTime**
5 minutes

**Pantry Raid**
Frying pan, small mixing bowl,
7"x 9" or larger microwave-safe
baking dish, plastic wrap, spatula

**Grocery Guide**
2 sole or flounder fillets
   (8 oz.–10 oz. total)—fresh or
   thawed in refrigerator
2 tsp. sesame seeds
Freshly ground black pepper

*For the sauce:*
1 Tb. sesame oil
2 tsp. soy sauce
1 tsp. lemon juice
1 garlic clove, peeled and minced
1 tsp. fresh ginger, peeled and
   minced

**Platemates**
24-Carat Carrots (page 83) and
   Top 40 Potatoes (page 85)

**F.Y.I.**
* *Seafood Doneness Check*:
   Serve when flesh inside
   thickest part of fish is slightly
   opaque, and flakes into natural
   divisions when probed with a
   fork.
* You can substitute any other
   delicate white fish fillets for the
   sole or flounder.

**No-Whine Wine Guide**
White Graves or Muscadet

**1** In an un-oiled frying pan on low heat, add sesame seeds and stir until lightly toasted, about 1-2 minutes. Remove from heat.

**2** *For the sauce:* Into mixing bowl, stir sesame oil, soy sauce, lemon juice, garlic and ginger.

**3** Into baking dish, arrange fillets in a single layer with thickest parts to the outside. Stir sauce and spoon over fillets. Season lightly with pepper. Cover dish loosely—or with plastic wrap leaving one corner open to vent.

**4** Microwave on High (100%) for 2 minutes. Turn dish and microwave on High till done, 1-2 minutes more (see Doneness Check).

**5** Carefully transfer fillets to dinner plates, spoon sauce over fish and sprinkle with toasted sesame seeds. Serve hot!

# Ginger Dijon Chicken
## *Pardon me, could you pass the Grey Poupon?*

---

*PrepTime*    *CookTime*
15 minutes    18 minutes

**Pantry Raid**
Plastic wrap, flat mallet or small saucepan, wide rimmed plate, 10"-12" non-stick frying pan, non-metal spatula, aluminum foil

**Grocery Guide**
¼ cup all-purpose flour
¼ tsp. salt
½ tsp. freshly ground black pepper
2 whole chicken breasts, skinned, boned and split in half
2 Tb. butter or margarine
¾ cup chicken broth (from bouillon cube or can)
1-2 tsp. fresh ginger, peeled and minced
1 Tb. + 1 tsp. coarse-grained Dijon mustard
4 green onions (bulb plus 2 inches of green), finely chopped

**F.Y.I.**
* *Chicken Doneness Check:* Chicken is no longer pink when slashed with a knife at the thickest part.
* For a change of taste, mix 3-4 minced pecans into the flour in Step 2.
* If your frying pan is too small to hold all the chicken in a single layer, cook in two batches.

**1** Place chicken breasts, one at a time, between 2 sheets of plastic wrap. With a flat mallet or bottom of small saucepan, gently pound until each is about ¼-inch thick.

**2** In rimmed plate, mix flour, salt and pepper. Dip breasts into flour to coat all sides evenly. Set aside.

**3** In frying pan, melt butter at medium heat, tilting pan to coat bottom. Add breasts in single layer and fry 4 minutes, loosening with spatula after 1 minute. Flip and fry breasts till they're completely cooked, about 4 minutes (see Doneness Check). Transfer to dinner plates, cover with aluminum foil to keep warm, and set aside.

**4** Increase heat to medium-high, pour chicken broth into frying pan and bring to boil. Add the ginger. With the spatula, scrape bottom of pan to stir in browned chicken pieces. Boil until the volume of liquid is reduced by half, 6-8 minutes.

**5** Mix in mustard and green onions and season lightly with additional salt and pepper. Stir 1 minute more.

**6** Spoon sauce equally over breasts. Serve immediately!

---

**No-Whine Wine Guide**
Pinot Blanc or Dry Gewürztraminer

**Platemates**
The Wildest Rice You Ever Ate
(page 87)

# $\mathcal{H}$oney Broiled Flank Steak
## Brings out the carnivore in your honey.

SERVES 2-4

**PrepTime**
10 minutes

**CookTime**
8-10 minutes

**Pantry Raid**
Chef's knife, baking pan (close-fitting to size of steak), plastic wrap, broiler pan, tongs, oven mitt, cutting board or platter with juice well

**Grocery Guide**
1 flank steak, about 1½ lbs.
¼-½ cup soy sauce
1 large garlic clove, peeled and minced
1 Tb. honey
¼ tsp. freshly ground black pepper

**Platemates**
Crispy Oven Potatoes (page 83) and a garden salad

**F.Y.I.**
✳ *Steak Doneness Check:* Meat is ready when its color is to your liking when slashed at the thickest portion.
✳ Leftovers make fine sandwiches the next day. Great in fajitas, too!

**No-Whine Wine Guide**
Cabernet Sauvignon or full-flavored Rhone

**1** *Thirty minutes to 24 hours ahead of time:* Unroll steak and score both sides in a crisscross pattern with cuts ⅛-inch deep and 1-inch apart.

**2** Place steak into baking pan and pour in enough soy sauce to barely cover steak. Rub top of steak with garlic, drizzle with honey and top with pepper.

**3** Gently flip steak over and shift it around in liquid for 1 minute. Flip it back over, cover with plastic wrap and refrigerate up to 24 hours.

**4** *When ready to cook:* Line broiler pan with aluminum foil to save messy clean-up. Set oven rack to level where top of meat will be 2-3 inches from heat source. Set oven to broil and preheat broiler pan.

**5** Remove steak from marinade and place on hot broiler rack. Broil 4 minutes, turn with tongs and broil 4 minutes longer for medium-rare—or continue broiling till meat is done to your liking (see Doneness Check).

**6** Transfer steak to carving platter. Slant knife diagonally and carve across the grain into ⅛" to ¼"-thick slices. Drizzle with pan juices and serve.

# Orange-Glazed Cornish Hens
*Oh those wild irresistible chicks.*

### PrepTime
15 minutes

### CookTime
55 minutes

### Pantry Raid
Medium-sized saucepan with cover, paper towels, frying pan, 9"x13" baking pan, oven mitts, bulb baster or large spoon, small mixing bowl

### Grocery Guide
¼ cup uncooked couscous
1 Tb. butter or margarine
1 small onion, finely chopped
2 tsp. curry powder
2 oz. shelled walnuts, coarsely chopped
4 garlic cloves, peeled and crushed
2 Tb. raisins
1 11-oz. can mandarin orange segments, drained and juice reserved
2 Rock Cornish game hens, 1-1¼ lb. each, fresh or thawed
Vegetable oil
2 Tb. orange marmalade
1 tsp. Dijon mustard
Salt and freshly ground black pepper

### F.Y.I.
∗ *Rock Cornish Game Hen Doneness Check:* When leg joint moves easily, birds are done.

**1** Prepare couscous according to directions on package. Meanwhile, remove packet of innards from inside hens. Rinse hens, pat dry with paper towels and sprinkle cavities with salt and pepper. Set aside.

**2** *Prepare the stuffing:* In frying pan at medium heat, melt butter, tilting pan to coat bottom. Add onions and curry and sauté 4 minutes. Add couscous to frying pan and mix with walnuts, garlic, raisins and half the mandarin orange segments. Remove from heat.

**3** Stuff the cavity of each hen equally with couscous mixture. Preheat oven to 375⁰. Coat bottom of baking pan with vegetable oil and add hens, legs-up. Brush hens lightly with vegetable oil and season lightly with salt and pepper.

**4** Bake hens uncovered for 25 minutes and baste with reserved orange juice. Bake 25 minutes more, basting hens every 6-7 minutes.

**5** In small bowl, mix marmalade and mustard and coat hens with mixture. Add remaining mandarin oranges to pan and return hens to oven till they're done, 5-10 minutes (see Doneness Check). Transfer to serving plates, top with orange segments from pan and serve hot and whole.

**No-Whine Wine Guide**
Chenin Blanc or Riesling

**Platemates**
Sesame Snow Peas (page 86), navel orange, quartered

# Good Luck Chicken
*Works like a charm.*

---

**PrepTime**
15 minutes

**CookTime**
30 minutes

**Pantry Raid**
Large frying pan with cover, slotted spoon, aluminum foil

**Grocery Guide**
3 Tb. butter or margarine
2 whole chicken breasts, boned, skinned and split in half
14 oz. can unmarinated artichoke hearts, drained
10-12 medium-sized fresh mushrooms, wiped clean and thinly sliced
1 large shallot, peeled and chopped
2 garlic cloves, peeled and minced
1 cup dry white wine
Salt and freshly ground pepper
1 Tb. all-purpose flour

**Platemates**
Crispy Oven Potatoes (page 83)

**F.Y.I.**
\* *Chicken Doneness Check:*
Chicken is no longer pink when slashed with a knife at the thickest part.

**No-Whine Wine Guide**
Sauvignon Blanc or Mâcon-Villages

**1** Melt 2 Tb. butter in frying pan on medium heat, tilting pan to coat bottom. Add chicken breasts in single layer and lightly brown on one side, about 4 minutes. Flip and repeat. With slotted spoon, transfer breasts to clean plate and set aside.

**2** In frying pan, melt remaining 1 Tb. butter. Add artichoke hearts and sauté 4 minutes. Transfer artichokes to plate with chicken.

**3** Add mushrooms, shallots and garlic to pan. Sauté 4 minutes. Return chicken and artichokes to pan in a single layer. Pour in wine and season lightly with salt and pepper. Reduce heat to low, cover and simmer 7-10 minutes, or until chicken is done (see Doneness Check).

**4** Meanwhile, in a small cup, dissolve 1 Tb. flour in 1 Tb. water and set aside.

**5** When chicken is done, use slotted spoon to transfer chicken and vegetables to warm serving platter. Cover with aluminum foil to keep warm.

**6** Add flour paste to liquid in frying pan and stir to thicken, about 3 minutes. Pour sauce over chicken and serve immediately!

# Spicy Three-Cheese Pizza
## *Guaranteed delivery in 28 minutes or less!*

Seize 'Em Salad (page 55)

### PrepTime
10 minutes

### CookTime
28 minutes

### Pantry Raid
Medium-sized saucepan with cover, frying pan, pizza pan or cookie sheet, pastry brush, pizza cutter

### Grocery Guide
1 12-inch store-bought pizza dough or crust
1 Tb. butter or margarine

*For the sauce:*
1 cup of your favorite tomato sauce
2 garlic cloves, peeled and crushed
1 Tb. dried basil
2 tsp. oregano
1 tsp. crushed red pepper flakes
1 tsp. olive oil or other cooking oil

*For the topping:*
8 medium-sized mushrooms, wiped clean and sliced
½ cup shredded mozzarella cheese
½ cup crumbled feta cheese
⅓ cup grated Parmesan cheese

### Platemates
Seize 'Em Salad (page 55)

### No-Whine Wine Guide
Côtes du Rhône or Red Zinfandel

**1** Add all the sauce ingredients plus 1 Tb. water to the saucepan, cover and simmer at the lowest possible heat for 20 minutes. Stir occasionally.

**2** Meanwhile, in frying pan on medium heat, melt butter, tilting the pan to coat bottom. Add mushrooms and sauté 3 minutes. Remove from heat and set aside.

**3** Prepare dough according to directions on package or brush oil lightly on top of crust. Oil pizza pan, place crust on pan and spread top of crust evenly with tomato sauce, leaving a ½-inch margin around the edge. Preheat oven to 450º.

**4** Sprinkle the mozzarella and feta cheeses evenly over the sauce. Spread mushrooms evenly, then sprinkle with Parmesan cheese. Bake uncovered till cheese is bubbly and edge of crust is golden, 7 minutes or more (depending on thickness of crust).

**5** To keep crust from getting soggy, slide it onto a cutting board when you remove it from the oven. Slice with pizza cutter or knife into 6 wedges and serve hot.

### F.Y.I.
* *Keep It Meatless:* Try adding some of these toppings for tasty variations: Lightly sautéed strips of green, red and/or yellow bell peppers, lightly sautéed onion rings, sliced green or ripe olives.
* *For Those Carnivores:* Top with pepperoni slices or fully-cooked sliced sweet or hot Italian sausage.

77

# Sensational Sideshows

*Earn Standing Ovations*
*With Simply Irresistible*
*Side Dishes*

*e*legant side dishes add variety, color and balance to your dinner. And they supplement your minimum daily adult requirements for vitamins, iron, fiber—and good taste.

Be sure to choose your side dishes carefully. Soggy brussel sprouts and boiled kale may stir up queasy childhood memories of his tantrums at the dinner table.

Try these nominees for best performance in supporting roles. Or some of them may be doubled and turned into grand entrees.

# Confetti Rice
*Turns any dinner into a celebration.*

SERVES 2

**PrepTime**
6 minutes

**CookTime**
25 minutes

**Pantry Raid**
Medium-sized saucepan with cover, grater

**Grocery Guide**
1 Tb. butter or margarine
½ cup uncooked converted white rice
1 fresh lemon, finely grated and cut in half
1 chicken bouillon cube
¾ cup finely chopped broccoli florets, carrots and/or zucchini
Dash white pepper

**1** In medium saucepan over low heat, melt butter and stir in rice and grated lemon peel. Increase heat to medium and stir till rice is translucent, 2-3 minutes

**2** Pour in 1⅓ cups water, add bouillon cube and bring to boil. Stir to dissolve cube. Reduce heat to low, cover and simmer about 20 minutes, or until all liquid is absorbed.

**3** Squeeze juice from half the lemon into rice, add vegetables and cover. Simmer 5 more minutes, stirring occasionally. Season lightly with white pepper.

**F.Y.I.**
\* When grating the lemon, don't grate into the bitter white pith underneath the peel.

# Magic Skillet Mushrooms
*They'll cast a spell on you.*

SERVES 2

**1** Slice off woody stem ends and cut mushrooms in half.

**2** In frying pan, melt butter over high heat. Immediately add mushrooms and stir or shake frying pan till mushrooms are lightly browned, 2-3 minutes. If a lot of water is released, stir-fry 2-3 minutes more till most water is evaporated. Reduce heat to medium.

**3** Add red wine and simmer and stir for 2 minutes. Stir in cream and simmer 2 minutes more. Lightly season with salt and pepper and serve.

**F.Y.I.**
\* *Sponge Warning:* Avoid rinsing mushrooms since they absorb water. Wipe them clean with a damp paper towel instead.

**PrepTime**
5 minutes

**CookTime**
3-6 minutes

**Pantry Raid**
10"-12" frying pan, paring knife, paper towels

**Grocery Guide**
½ lb. medium-sized fresh mushrooms, wiped clean
3 Tb. butter or margarine
2 Tb. red wine
1 Tb. sour cream or heavy cream
Salt and freshly ground pepper

# Nutty Green Beans
*Chop till you drop.*

**PrepTime**    **CookTime**
5 minutes    5 minutes

**Pantry Raid**
Medium-sized saucepan with
cover, paring knife, frying pan

**Grocery Guide**
½ lb. green beans, rinsed and
   ends trimmed
2 Tb. butter or margarine
3 Tb. chopped pecans
Pinch nutmeg
Salt and freshly ground black
   pepper

**F.Y.I.**
✱ Toasted pine nuts or almonds
   are a nutty alternative.

**1** Pour water into saucepan till it's half filled and add ½ tsp. salt. Bring to boil on medium heat, add beans and cook till crisp-tender, about 5 minutes.

**2** Drain off boiling water with lid and immediately pour cold water over beans. Drain again and set aside.

**3** In frying pan at medium heat, melt butter, tilting pan to coat bottom. As soon as butter begins to sizzle, add pecans and stir-fry till butter is nut-brown and foam subsides. Stir beans into nut butter, remove from heat and season lightly with nutmeg, salt and pepper.

# Dill-icious Potatoes
*Dill out and dig in.*

**1** Scrub potatoes and prick each one with a fork. Place in microwave 1 inch apart and zap on High (100%) for 7-10 minutes, or till tender when pierced with a fork.

**2** Cut potatoes into quarters (leave skin on) and place in mixing bowl.

**3** Mix together with sour cream and dill and season lightly with salt and pepper.

**PrepTime**
2 minutes
**CookTime**
10 minutes
**Pantry Raid**
Medium-sized mixing bowl
**Grocery Guide**
1 lb. New potatoes, all a similar
   size
¼ cup sour cream or plain (not
   vanilla) yogurt
1½ Tb. fresh dill weed, chopped
   (or ½ Tb. dried dill weed)
Salt and freshly ground pepper

# Rock Me Broccoli
*The special of the day at the Hard Broc Café.*

SERVES 2

### PrepTime
6 minutes

### CookTime
4 minutes

### Pantry Raid
Microwave-safe dish, plastic wrap, grater, peeler

### Grocery Guide
½ lb. fresh broccoli
1 Tb. butter or margarine, softened to room temperature
1 Tb. shelled walnuts, minced
½ Tb. dry bread crumbs
½ tsp. finely grated lemon peel
Salt and freshly ground pepper

**1** Rinse broccoli and cut tops into bite-sized florets. Peel stems and cut crosswise into ¼-inch coins.

**2** Place florets and coins in microwave-safe dish and add 2 Tb. water. Cover loosely with plastic wrap and microwave on High (100%) for 3 minutes, or till florets are bright green. Pour off liquid.

**3** Add butter and stir till melted. Mix in walnuts, bread crumbs and lemon peel. Cover and zap on High 1 minute more, season lightly with salt and pepper and serve.

### F.Y.I.
* When grating the lemon, don't grate into the bitter white pith underneath the peel.

---

# Hot Saga Bread
*Go gaga over saga.*

SERVES 4-6

**1** Preheat oven to 350°. Slice bread down the middle into 2 long halves.

**2** Spread the butter equally on each half. Spread the cheese—rind and all—down one of the halves.

**3** Place halves together, wrap in foil and place in oven for 20-25 minutes. Slice and serve.

### F.Y.I.
* For 2 portions, use 2 baguettes and half the ingredients.

### PrepTime
5 minutes

### CookTime
20-25 minutes

### Pantry Raid
Serrated bread knife, aluminum foil

### Grocery Guide
Fresh loaf of French bread
¼ cup butter or margarine, softened to room temperature
½ lb. saga blue or *bleu de bresse* cheese, softened to room temperature

# 24-Carat Carrots
*A hungry girl's best friend.*

---

**PrepTime**
5 minutes

**CookTime**
12 minutes

**Pantry Raid**
Small saucepan with cover

**Grocery Guide**
3-4 medium-sized carrots, peeled
12-16 oz. unsweetened pineapple
  juice
1 Tb. orange marmalade or
  apricot preserves
1 Tb. butter or margarine,
  softened to room temperature
¼ tsp. white pepper

**1** Cut peeled carrots diagonally into ¼-inch coins.

**2** Add carrots to saucepan and pour in pineapple juice till carrots are submerged. Cover and boil at medium heat 8-10 minutes, or till carrots are tender when pierced with a fork. Remove cover and boil 3 minutes more, stirring often to evaporate about half the juice.

**3** Stir in marmalade and butter. Reduce heat to low and simmer until carrots are nicely glazed, stirring occasionally. Season with white pepper.

**F.Y.I.**
✱ For a change of taste, substitute orange or grapefruit juice in Step 2.
✱ For added zing, add a pinch of dried dill weed to sauce in Step 3.

---

# Crispy Oven Potatoes
*Tasty spuds for your buds.*

SERVES 2

---

**1** If potatoes are larger than golf ball-size, cut in half or quarters (do not peel). With a paper towel, lightly coat potatoes with olive oil and place in baking pan. Preheat oven to 400º.

**2** Bake uncovered for 40 minutes, or till potatoes pierce easily with a fork. Set oven to Broil for 1 minute to crisp potatoes.

**3** Transfer potatoes to bowl, add 1 Tb. butter, thyme and season lightly with salt and pepper. Mix well to coat. Serve.

**F.Y.I.**
✱ For an added dimension, sprinkle with grated Parmesan or Romano cheese in Step 3.

**PrepTime**     **CookTime**
5 minutes       40 minutes

**Pantry Raid**
8"-square baking pan, paper towels, medium-sized mixing bowl

**Grocery Guide**
6 small Red or New potatoes,
  scrubbed and dried
2 Tb. olive oil
1 Tb. butter or margarine,
  softened to room temperature
½ tsp. thyme
Salt and freshly ground pepper

# Golden Garlic Bread
## Garlic-ety split!

**PrepTime**
5 minutes

**CookTime**
20 minutes

**Pantry Raid**
Serrated bread knife, small mixing bowl, aluminum foil

**Grocery Guide**
Fresh loaf of Italian or French bread
3-4 garlic cloves, peeled and crushed
¼ cup butter or margarine, softened to room temperature

**1** Preheat oven to 350°. Slice bread down the middle into 2 long halves.

**2** In small bowl, mash butter and garlic together. Smear insides of bread with garlic-butter. Close bread and cut loaf into 1-inch slices, not quite through to the bottom.

**3** Wrap bread in foil, place on baking sheet in hot oven for 15 minutes. Carefully remove bread from foil and bake 4-5 more minutes to crisp bread.

### F.Y.I.
* Do yourself a flavor and add ½ tsp. *each* of dried basil, oregano and marjoram at Step 2.
* A small jar of pre-crushed garlic makes this job a snap!
* For 2 portions, use 2 baguettes and half the ingredients.

# Boogie Woogie Broccoli
## You'll wanna rock around the clock.

SERVES 2

**1** Pour 1 inch of water into saucepan and bring to boil on medium heat. Add vegetables to steamer basket and place steamer in pan. Cover and steam till vegetables are crisp-tender, 4-6 minutes.

**2** Place vegetables on serving plates and drizzle with lemon juice.

**PrepTime**          **CookTime**
6 minutes            4-6 minutes

**Pantry Raid**
Vegetable steamer, medium saucepan with cover

**Grocery Guide**
¼ lb. broccoli, rinsed and cut into bite-sized florets
¼ lb. cauliflower, rinsed and cut into bite-sized florets
1 small red bell pepper, rinsed, top and seeds removed, cut into thin rings
2 tsp. lemon juice

# Shredded Carrots a l'Orange
## *Less filing. Tastes grate.*

**PrepTime**    **CookTime**
8 minutes    4 minutes

**Pantry Raid**
Frying pan, grater

**Grocery Guide**
2 Tb. butter or margarine
4 medium-sized carrots, peeled
   and coarsely grated
1 navel orange, outer peel grated,
   cut in half
1 tsp. sugar
Dash nutmeg
Salt and freshly ground pepper

**1** In frying pan over high heat, melt butter. Quickly add grated carrots and grated peel and stir-fry 2 minutes.

**2** Squeeze orange halves over carrots, add sugar and continue stir-frying until liquid is almost absorbed, about 2 minutes. Remove from heat.

**3** Add nutmeg and season lightly with salt and pepper. Serve hot.

**F.Y.I.**
* When grating the orange, don't grate into the bitter white pith underneath the peel.

---

# Top 40 Potatoes
## *A real chart-buster!*

SERVES 2

**1** Scrub potatoes well and pierce in several places with fork.

**2** Microwave on High (100%) for 6-7 minutes. Turn potatoes once during cooking. Careful. . .they're hot!

**3** Meanwhile, mix sauce ingredients in mixing bowl. When potatoes are ready, slice open and spoon sauce on top.

**F.Y.I.**
* For added zest, mix ¼ tsp. crushed red pepper flakes into the sauce.
* When grating the lemon, don't grate into the bitter white pith underneath the peel.

**PrepTime**
4 minutes

**CookTime**
6-7 minutes

**Pantry Raid**
Small mixing bowl, grater, fork

**Grocery Guide**
2 baking potatoes

*For the sauce:*
½ cup plain (not vanilla) yogurt
1 Tb. lemon juice
¼ tsp. finely grated lemon peel
2 green onions (bulb plus
   2 inches of green), finely chopped
1 small garlic clove, peeled and
   crushed

85

# Sesame Snow Peas
## Go stir crazy!

*PrepTime*
3 minutes

*CookTime*
4 minutes

*Pantry Raid*
Paper towels, frying pan, spatula

*Grocery Guide*
¼ lb. snow peas
1 tsp. sesame seeds
1 tsp. sesame oil
Salt and freshly ground pepper

**1** Rinse snow peas and pull off ends. Pat dry on paper towels and set aside.

**2** In a non-oiled frying pan on low heat, add sesame seeds and stir-fry until lightly toasted, 1-2 minutes. Don't let 'em burn! Remove from pan and set aside. Allow pan to cool for 2 minutes.

**3** Heat oil in frying pan over medium-high heat. When oil is sizzling hot, add snow peas and stir-fry till they turn bright green, 1½-2 minutes. Transfer to dinner plates, sprinkle equally with toasted sesame seeds and season lightly with salt and pepper.

# New Potatoes Rosemarie
## Smile a little smile for me. . .

SERVES 4

**1** Heat olive oil in frying pan on low heat. Add garlic, stir-fry 4 minutes, remove with spoons and set aside.

**2** Add potatoes and sprinkle with salt, pepper and half the rosemary. Stir to coat. Cover, increase heat to medium and fry till potatoes are tender when pierced with a fork, 10-12 minutes. Stir occasionally.

**3** Increase heat to high and stir till potatoes are browned, 3-4 minutes. Remove from heat, return garlic to pan and toss with remaining ½ tsp. rosemary. Season with additional salt and pepper to your liking.

*PrepTime*
5 minutes

*CookTime*
20 minutes

*Pantry Raid*
10"-12" frying pan with cover, spatula

*Grocery Guide*
2 Tb. olive oil
2 garlic cloves, peeled and minced
6 small New potatoes, scrubbed
  and cut in quarters
½ tsp. salt
¼ tsp. freshly ground black
  pepper
1 tsp. dried rosemary leaves,
  crumbled

# The Wildest Rice You Ever Ate
*Take a walk on the wild side.*

**PrepTime**
4 minutes

**CookTime**
25-30 minutes

**Pantry Raid**
Medium-sized saucepan with cover

**Grocery Guide**
1 small box of herb-seasoned wild rice
1 Tb. butter or margarine
½ cup chopped pecan pieces
½ cup raisins

**1** Follow directions on wild rice package for 4 portions.

**2** Five minutes before rice is ready, stir in chopped pecans and raisins.

**3** Cover and continue cooking the final 5 minutes, or until all water is absorbed and rice is tender. Stir before serving.

---

SERVES 3-4

# Minty Potatoes
*A fresh twist on an old spud.*

**1** Place potatoes in saucepan and add enough water to immerse them completely. Stir in ½ tsp. salt.

**2** Set heat to medium and bring to boil. Cook uncovered till potatoes are tender when pierced with a fork (about 10 minutes after water boils).

**3** Use cover to drain water into sink. Mix potatoes with butter and mint leaves and season lightly with salt and pepper. Cover. Potatoes will stay hot until the rest of your meal is ready.

**PrepTime**
5 minutes

**CookTime**
15 minutes

**Pantry Raid**
Medium saucepan with cover

**Grocery Guide**
1 lb. small New potatoes, scrubbed
2 Tb. butter or margarine, melted
1 Tb. chopped fresh mint leaves
Salt and freshly ground pepper

CHAPTER 12

# Sweet Sinsations

*Desserts Guaranteed To Satisfy Everyone's Sweet Teeth*

And now, the moment you've been waiting for—dessert!

Cook up these sinful treats and you're sure to win your guest's growing affections. But beware: Too much pre-tasting, bowl-licking and chocolate chip nibbling can ruin your masterpiece, your appetite *and* your waistline.

## Ice Cream Mix-Ins & Fixin's

Open up an ice cream parlor in your living room! Just nuke your ice cream on Medium (50%) for half a minute to soften it, and get ready to get mixin'!

**Three Berry Surprise**
Marinate blueberries and sliced strawberries in Grand Marnier in the refrigerator. Spoon over scoops of strawberry ice cream and sprinkle with almond slivers.

**Espresso Thyself**
Sprinkle instant espresso powder over a scoop of chocolate chip ice cream.

**Womanwich**
Take two big oatmeal cookies and make an ice cream sandwich with one scoop of maple walnut ice cream. Then roll the edges around in chopped walnuts.

**Peachy Ginger Snap**
Grind up a few ginger cookies and mash into vanilla ice cream. Top with fresh peach slices.

## Easy No-Cook Desserts

Too busy to bake? Try these one-step desserts and savor a little low-fat heaven on earth.

### It's A Grape Life
Mix rinsed, seedless grapes with your favorite low-fat yogurt and spoon into wine glasses. Dust with brown sugar and chill. *Voila!*

### J.C. Melloncup
Add chilled watermelon, honeydew and cantaloupe balls to champagne glasses. Drizzle with kirsch or fruit brandy.

### Loupe d'Loupe
Slice a ripe cantaloupe in half, scoop out seeds and replace with fresh blueberries, blackberries or raspberries.

### Cup-A-Fruit
Before dinner, place sliced strawberries, sliced pineapple chunks and seedless green grapes in a bowl. Dust with sugar, drizzle with Cointreau and stir. Chill for an after-dinner treat.

### Orange Orange
Peel oranges and cut into wedges. Place in wine glasses, drizzle with Grand Marnier and chill.

### Fruit 'n' Cheese
Pass around some fresh whole fruit with cheese wedges for a winning combo. Try cheddar, Swiss or Monterey Jack with pears, apples, seedless grapes or honeydew. Brie or Camembert with peaches, plums or pineapple. Fontina or port du salut with cantaloupe. Or neufchatel with strawberries or watermelon.

## Triple Decadence
### Three sins—no waiting!

SERVES 2

2 large, fresh bakery brownies
2 big scoops premium vanilla ice
   cream
1½ oz. Kahlua
Whipped cream

**1** You know what to do.

## Parfait Accompli
### Made with the greatest of ease.

SERVES 2

1 small can pineapple chunks,
   drained
1 Tb. honey
2 scoops strawberry ice cream
2 scoops vanilla ice cream
Whipped cream

*Important Extras:*
2 Maraschino cherries
Handful of chocolate jimmies

**1** In small mixing bowl, stir pineapple chunks and honey.

**2** In 2 parfait or pilsner glasses, layer the ingredients: scoop of strawberry ice cream, pineapple mixture, vanilla ice cream, pineapple mixture. Top with whipped cream, jimmies and cherry.

## Sap Zap Sundae
### It'll meltdown his heart.

SERVES 2

½ cup real maple syrup
¼ cup shelled walnuts
2-4 scoops vanilla and/or coffee ice
   cream

*Important Extras:*
2 Maraschino cherries

**1** Mix maple syrup and walnuts in small, microwave-safe bowl. Microwave on High (100%) for 30 seconds or till warm.

**2** Meanwhile, spoon ice cream into two dessert bowls. Spoon warm walnut-syrup over top. Mmmmmmm!

## Plum Smoothy
### It's ripe 'n' ready!

SERVES 2

2 ripe purple plums, pits removed
1 ripe Bartlett pear, cored
½ cup vanilla low-fat yogurt
1 Tb. sugar
4 ice cubes

## Peachy Keen
### A perfect blend of amaretto and amore.

SERVES 2

1 cup peeled, sliced peaches
2 Tb. amaretto
2 amaretti cookies, crushed

**1** Place peach slices in microwave-safe dessert cups. Drizzle amaretto over peaches. Cover with plastic wrap.

**2** Microwave on High (100%) for 1 minute. Remove plastic wrap and sprinkle cookie crumbs over hot peaches. Serve!

**1** Put everything in blender. Turn it on. Dessert's ready when it's plum smoothy! Pour into wine glasses. Cheers!

91

# Blueberry Ribbons

*A real prize winner!*

SERVES 4

¼ cup sugar
1 Tb. cornstarch
12 oz. bag frozen blueberries
1 tsp. lemon juice
1 pint vanilla ice cream

**1** In medium-sized microwave-safe mixing bowl, stir sugar and cornstarch together. Add blueberries and stir. Microwave on High (100%) for 4 minutes. Stir 1 tsp. lemon juice into blueberry sauce.

**2** Into each tall dessert glass spoon 2 Tb. of blueberry sauce. Follow with ½ scoop of ice cream, then more sauce and another ½ scoop ice cream. Finally, pour remaining sauce over top and serve!

# Flaming Bananas

*Sounds like a rock 'n' roll band. Tastes like heaven.*

SERVES 2

1 tsp. butter (not margarine)
1 tsp. honey
⅛ tsp. ground nutmeg
1 slightly underripe, banana, peeled and cut in half lengthwise
1 Tb. chopped pecans
2 Tb. dark rum

**1** In microwave-safe 12 oz. casserole dish, microwave butter on High (100%) for 20 seconds or until melted.

**2** Stir in honey and nutmeg. Coat banana in honey mixture and sprinkle with pecans. Zap till hot, 30-60 seconds on High and remove from microwave.

**3** Meanwhile, pour rum into microwave-safe cup. Zap on High for 15 seconds. Pour heated rum into metal ladle, ignite with match, and pour flaming liquid over hot bananas. Perfect!

# Sin-Dipped Strawberries

*The devil's downfall.*

SERVES 2

4 oz. semi-sweet chocolate chips
2 Tb. rum
⅓ lb. fresh strawberries, rinsed and patted dry

**1** Add chocolate and rum to small microwave-safe mixing bowl. Microwave on High for 2 minutes. Stir.

**2** Hold strawberries by stems and dip in chocolate, lay on wax paper and chill till hard, 10-15 minutes.

# Pineapple Head-Over-Heels Cake
*They'll flip at first bite.*

¼ cup butter or margarine
½ cup brown sugar
6 pineapple slices
10 cherries, pitted
½ cup pecan halves
18 oz. package of
    yellow cake mix

**1** Preheat oven to 350º. Melt butter in cake layer pan or 8"x 8" baking pan over very low heat. Spoon brown sugar over butter. Play food stylist and arrange the pineapple slices, cherries and pecans over mixture (remember, it'll be upside-down!).

**2** Prepare cake mix according to directions on package, but pour only half of the batter over fruit (freeze the rest for another date).

**3** Bake 35-40 minutes. It's done when a toothpick inserted in the center comes out clean. Remove from oven and let cool 10 minutes.

**4** To remove cake from pan, run a knife around the edge of cake. Place serving platter on top of pan, hold tight and flip. Tap bottom. Wait a few moments. Lift off pan. *Voila!*

# Tropical Island Treat
*It's a vacation sensation.*

SERVES 2

**1** In baking pan, arrange pineapple slices in single layer. Pour Grand Marnier and sprinkle brown sugar evenly over slices.

**2** Turn on broiler. Place baking pan 4-6 inches from heat for about 4 minutes, or until sugar is bubbling and golden. Remove pan with oven mitt and transfer slices to dessert dishes. Place cherries in center of pineapple and serve hot!

4 thick slices of fresh pineapple,
    pared and cored
1 Tb. brown sugar
1 tsp. Grand Marnier
4 Maraschino cherries

# Cherries Jubilee
## *Dim the lights and light the fuse.*

¼ cup sugar
1 Tb. cornstarch
1 can (1 lb. 13 oz.) pitted Bing
   cherries in syrup
1 Tb. lemon juice
1 Tb. butter
⅓ cup kirsch or brandy
Vanilla ice cream

**1** Add sugar and cornstarch to medium saucepan. Set burner to medium heat and slowly mix in syrup from cherries while continuously stirring. Bring to boil, then set to simmer for 3 minutes, stirring once a minute. Then add lemon juice, butter and cherries. Simmer 3 minutes.

**2** Meanwhile, add kirsch to small saucepan. Set burner to low and warm liquid.

**3** Pour cherry mixture into flameproof dessert bowl and top with warm kirsch. Dim house lights, ignite mixture with match and carefully bring bowl to table. Spoon over vanilla ice cream in dessert bowls and take a bow.

# Honey Pear Crumble
## *This will sweet-talk 'em into anything.*

SERVES 4

**1** Preheat oven to 375º. In a mixing bowl, stir together pears, lemon juice and honey.

**2** Lightly coat an 8"x 8" baking pan or small casserole dish with butter. Pour in pear mixture and distribute evenly.

**3** In clean mixing bowl, stir flour, brown sugar, cinnamon, nutmeg, nuts and butter to form a crumbly mixture. Pour evenly over pear mixture—don't stir—and bake 35 minutes or until fruit is tender and topping is golden brown. Serve warm with ice cream or whipped topping.

3 ripe pears, peeled and cut
   ¼-inch thick
1 Tb. lemon juice
2½ Tb. honey
1 tsp. butter for coating pan
¼ cup all-purpose flour
⅓ cup brown sugar
½ tsp. cinnamon
¼ tsp. nutmeg
¼ cup chopped walnuts or pecans
2½ Tb. butter or margarine,
   softened and cut into chunks
Vanilla ice cream or whipped
   topping

## Decadent Dessert Drinks

Serve these hypnotic after-dinner libations with—or as—dessert!

### Chocolate Chip Cookie
Into a rocks glass with ice, mix ¾ oz. Frangelico with ¾ oz. dark creme de cacao and fill with cream.

### Nutty Irishman
Into a rocks glass with ice, mix ¾ oz. Bailey's Irish Creme with ¾ oz. Frangelico.

### Alcohol-Free!

### BananaRama
Into a blender add: 1 cup plain lowfat yogurt, 1 ripe banana cut into pieces, 2 Tb. honey and 3 ice cubes. Blend together till smooth. Serves 2.

### Sultry Hot Cider
Heat 2 cups cider with 1 Tb. honey, ¼ tsp. cinammon and ¼ tsp. cloves in a saucepan on medium heat. When it's hot, pour into mugs and garnish each with a cinammon stick. (*Optional:* add ⅓ cup apple brandy or Schnapps.)

## And here's more for amour!

✱ Liven up the evening with your favorite liqueur: Frangelico (hazelnut flavor from Italy), Tia Maria (coffee flavor from Jamaica) or Bailey's Original Irish Cream.

✱ Spice up a cold night with our Sultry Hot Cider.

✱ Perk him up with specialty coffee drinks (page 105).

✱ Celebrate the occasion with champagne.

✱ Or try any of these old faithfuls: coffee, tea, sweet wine, brandy or Diet Coke.

# CHAPTER 13
## Quick 'n' Dirty Pick Up Lines

*Seductive Reasoning
To Get Him To Do
The Dishes*

hhhhh. Dinner is over. The candles are flickering low. The compliments keep coming. And your stomachs are full.

Unfortunately, so is the sink.

Why, after all your work, should you find yourself back in the kitchen—alone—up to your elbows in dirty pots, pans and dishes? And why, after being treated like royalty, should he stay in the living room—alone—glued to the TV, buried in the sports page or deep in slumber?

What's wrong with this picture?

It seems that getting men to clean up nuclear waste is easier than getting them to help you clean

up the kitchen. But it doesn't have to be. Now you can stop them from taking advantage of your new domestic skills.

Try some of these proven pick up lines in your sexiest voice to lure him into the kitchen and lend you a hand. You'll finally put some fun into this dreaded chore.

97

# CHAPTER 14

# Arouse 'n' Shine

*Why Wait Till
Dark For Romance?*

*n*ow playing at your local breakfast bar: The All-American All-U-Can-Eat Brunch, featuring powdered eggs overcooking in an industrial-sized chafing dish. . .carbonized strips of bacon. . .greasy sausage links. . .rubber pancakes. . . cardboard muffins. . .flat champagne. Only $12.95 per person.

You can help yourself to acid indigestion, or you can fix a fantastic homecooked brunch away from the hungry hordes wallowing at the breakfast trough.

Never mind if it's his turn to treat you. Whip up one of the breakfast recipes in this chapter—and experience a morning of magic together.

If you have kids, pack 'em a Pop Tarts treat and send 'em out to play with the kids next door.

*You can help yourself to acid indigestion, or you can fix a fantastic homecooked brunch away from the hungry hordes wallowing at the breakfast trough.*

# The Ahhh-melet
## Open up and say ahhh....

### PrepTime
12 minutes

### CookTime
6 minutes

### Pantry Raid
Large non-stick frying pan, small and medium-sized mixing bowls, spatula

### Grocery Guide
4 large eggs
2 Tb. butter or margarine
½ medium-sized onion, diced
½ green bell pepper, rinsed, seeded and diced
½ medium-sized tomato, rinsed and diced
4 medium-sized mushrooms, wiped clean and sliced
⅓ cup grated sharp cheddar cheese
⅛ tsp. ground red cayenne pepper

### Platemates
Toasted bagels and cream cheese or toasted English muffins and strawberry jam

### F.Y.I.
✳ Allow eggs to come to room temperature before cooking, or cover them for a minute under hot tap water.

**1** Break eggs into medium-sized mixing bowl and add 1 Tb. water. Beat with fork just until yolks and whites are mixed.

**2** In frying pan on medium heat, melt 1 Tb. butter and add onions, green pepper, tomato and mushrooms and sauté 4 minutes. Transfer vegetables to small mixing bowl.

**3** Increase heat to medium-high and melt remaining 1 Tb. butter in frying pan. When butter is frothy-brown, pour in egg mixture. As edges quickly begin to set, gently lift with spatula and tilt pan to let uncooked egg flow underneath.

**4** When egg mixture no longer flows freely, quickly sprinkle with grated cheese and cayenne pepper. Then transfer all the vegetables onto the half of the omelet opposite the pan handle.

**5** Lift handle and tip pan down. With spatula, gently flip top half of omelet over bottom half. Slide folded omelet onto warm serving dish, cut omelet in half, garnish with fresh parsley and serve hot!

# Lovin' Oven Pancake
## It rises to the occasion.

*PrepTime*
6 minutes

*CookTime*
20 minutes

*Pantry Raid*
8½-inch round cake pan, mixing bowl, whisk, 2 spatulas, oven mitt

*Grocery Guide*
2 large eggs
1 cup all-purpose flour
1 cup milk
1 tsp. cinnamon
1 tsp. vanilla extract
2 Tb. chopped walnuts
Dash salt
2 Tb. butter or margarine
1 ripe banana, peeled and sliced
   into ¼-inch coins
Pancake syrup

*Platemates*
Flying Fruit Fantasy (page 105)
   and Keoki Coffee (page 105)

*F.Y.I.*
✳ Serve with *real* maple syrup,
   warmed.

**1** Break eggs into mixing bowl and whisk with flour, milk, cinnamon, vanilla, chopped walnuts and salt till mixture is smooth. Preheat oven to 375º.

**2** In pan, melt butter at low heat, tilting pan to coat bottom and sides. Don't let butter burn! Remove pan from heat.

**3** Slowly pour batter into center of pan—don't stir—and top evenly with banana slices. Place pan in center of oven and bake till it's puffy on the edges and golden brown on top, about 20 minutes.

**4** With two spatulas, carefully lift pancake from pan and place on serving plate. Cut into quarters and serve with pancake syrup and butter.

# *French Toast Très Terrifique*
## *The perfect way to say bonjour.*

### *PrepTime*
10 minutes

### *CookTime*
8 minutes

### *Pantry Raid*
Wide mixing bowl, 10" non-stick frying pan, non-metal spatula, grater, whisk

### *Grocery Guide*
2 large eggs
¼ cup milk
3 Tb. Grand Marnier or other
  orange liqueur
¼ tsp. cinnamon
¼ tsp. nutmeg
1 navel orange
Butter or margarine
2-4 slices day-old French or white
  bread, cut 1-inch thick
Maple syrup or confectioners'
  sugar

### *F.Y.I.*
✱ When grating the orange, don't
  grate into the bitter white pith
  underneath the peel.
✱ Try this dish with thick-cut
  cinnamon-raisin bread.

### *Platemates*
Warm 100% maple syrup
  (microwave 1 minute on High)
  and garnish plate with reserved
  orange slices.

**1** Break eggs into mixing bowl and whisk together with milk, liqueur, cinnamon and nutmeg.

**2** Rinse orange and pat dry. Cut orange in half, cut off 2 thin slices for garnish and set aside. Grate peel from half the orange into mixing bowl, squeeze juice from both halves into mixture (pick out any falling seeds) and whisk thoroughly.

**3** Melt 1 Tb. butter in frying pan on medium heat, tilting pan to coat bottom.

**4** Immediately dunk 1 bread slice in egg mixture, turning to coat both sides well. Transfer to hot frying pan. Repeat process with another bread slice and place in single layer in frying pan. Fry each side till golden brown, flip and repeat. Transfer to serving platter and keep warm. Repeat Steps 3 and 4 for another batch.

**5** Top with maple syrup or confectioners' sugar and garnish with orange slices.

# Go Nuts Banana Bread
## The taste will make you crazy!

**PrepTime**
15 minutes

**CookTime**
60 minutes

**Pantry Raid**
9"x5"x3" bread loaf pan, large mixing bowl, medium-sized mixing bowl

**Grocery Guide**
1 cup sugar
½ cup vegetable oil
2 eggs
3 ripe bananas, peeled and mashed
3 Tb. milk
2 cups all-purpose flour
1 tsp. baking soda
½ tsp. baking powder
Pinch salt
½ tsp. vanilla
½ cup chopped walnuts or pecans

**1** Lightly coat insides of bread loaf pan with oil. Add 1 tsp. flour into pan and tap till bottom and sides are lightly dusted. Preheat oven to 350º.

**2** In large mixing bowl, stir sugar and oil with fork. Whisk in eggs, bananas and milk till blended.

**3** In medium-sized mixing bowl, blend flour, baking soda, baking powder and salt. Spoon into banana mixture with vanilla and ⅔ of the nuts. Mix well and pour into loaf pan.

**4** Bake about 1 hour till loaf is springy to the touch. Cool upright in pan 10 minutes, then pop out of pan and cool on wire rack before slicing. Top with remaining nuts.

# Razzamatazzberry Fruit Bowl
*Cantaloupe you can't resist.*

SERVES 2

**PrepTime**
5 minutes

**Pantry Raid**
Fine sieve

**Grocery Guide**
10 oz. frozen raspberries in syrup, thawed

*Any one or combination of the following fruits, chilled:*
½ cantaloupe or honeydew melon, seeded and cut into quarter crescents
1 grapefruit, cut in half
2 navel oranges, sectioned

**1** Slice or section fruit as directed.

**2** Mash raspberries through a fine sieve with back of spoon. If raspberries are not in syrup, stir in 1 Tb. sugar.

**3** Arrange fruit on plates and pour raspberry sauce over fruit.

# Braguettes 'n' Yogurt
*Rip, dip and sip.*

SERVES 2

**1** Too tired to cook anything? Pick up a couple of fresh baguettes and a trio of premium yogurts. Tear the bread into pieces, dip in yogurt and sip with your favorite Perk-'Em-Up.

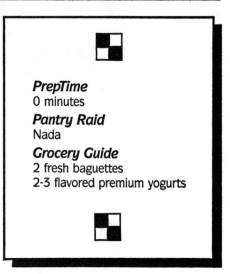

**PrepTime**
0 minutes

**Pantry Raid**
Nada

**Grocery Guide**
2 fresh baguettes
2-3 flavored premium yogurts

## Perk-'Em-Ups

Lift everyone's spirits with these eye-opening potions.

### Raspberries in Champagne
Rinse a few fresh raspberries and add to champagne flutes. Fill glass with champagne.

### Screwdriver
Mix 1 oz. vodka and fresh orange juice on ice. Stir. Serve in a wine glass and garnish with an orange slice.

### Grand Mimosa
Add ½ oz. Grand Marnier to chilled champagne containing enough orange juice to make it opaque. Serve in a wine glass over ice.

## Hot Wake-Up Calls

### Kahlua 'n' Caffeine
Add 1 oz. of Kahlua into a coffee mug. Fill with hot black coffee and top with whipped cream.

### Keoki Coffee
Pour ½ oz. brandy, ½ oz. dark creme de cacao and ½ oz. Kahlua into a coffee mug. Fill with hot black coffee, stir, and top with whipped cream.

### Dutch Coffee
Add 1 oz. chocolate mint liqueur into hot black coffee and top with whipped cream.

## No Buzz Wake-Up Calls

### Flying Fruit Fantasy
Cut up ½ cup of orange and melon slices. Place in two wine glasses and pour in chilled pineapple juice.

### Cranberry Berry Good
Place ice cubes in tall glass. Fill ⅔-way with cranberry juice. Add 1 tsp. lime juice and top with club soda. Stir.

# Congratulations!

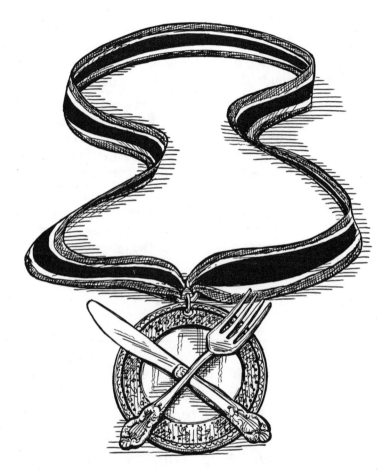

## GROUP MEALS AHEAD

*Now that you've earned the Busy Woman's Distinguished Service Cross and overcome Kitchen Performance Anxiety, cooking for the entire clan will be a piece of cake. Good luck!*

# CHAPTER 15

# Honor Thy Parents

### Or How To Host A Family Affair (Not A Family Feud)

Three thousand, five hundred and seventy? Seven thousand, one hundred and four? Nine thousand, six hundred and sixty five?

Your parents have cooked so many meals for you it's impossible to keep track. So don't you think it's time to reciprocate and present them with something special? Something not made from plaster of Paris or paper maché? Something other than a broken appliance, overdue bill or birthday wishlist?

Fair's fair. After all, you pigged out at their expense for years...and you still raid their fridge when you visit. Now's your chance to set a great scene instead of making one. Here's how to prepare a hearty, healthy full-course feast that shows them you don't live on junk food alone.

*Sure, you'll never even the score. But now you can do a lot better than carnations for Mother's Day, ties for Father's Day and a belated greeting card for their Anniversary!*

# good time guide #3:

## How To Prove You're All Grown Up Now

* Hide your diary and copies of "Nice Girls Do It," "My Secret Gardener" and "Mummy Dearest."

* Fix your hair, make your bed, stand up straight, find a nice rich man . . .

* Don't ask them to bring anything. Take care of them for a change.

* Don't talk back. And don't talk with your mouth full.

* Don't let your mother help in the kitchen. Save her offer for those times when you really need it—like when you come down with the flu.

* Refrain from snide remarks about your stupid siblings.

* Don't serve fattening desserts (or you can expect unwanted comments about your figure).

* Avoid getting defensive when Mom names other "girls" who (a) have gotten easier, higher-paying jobs (b) found perfect husbands, and (c) had adorable babies.

* Give your Mom a doggie bag's worth of solid bragging material about your career and social life.

* Insist they lock their car doors, drive safely and call you as soon as they get home.

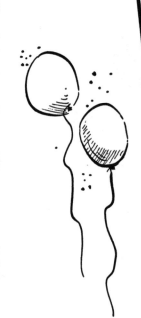

# Technicolor Pasta Salad
## Enjoy a full spectrum of flavor.

**PrepTime**   **CookTime**
20 minutes   15 minutes

**Pantry Raid**
Large pot, colander, steamer basket, frying pan with cover, large pasta bowl, vegetable peeler

**Grocery Guide**
- ½ lb. uncooked tri-color or plain rotini pasta
- 2 cups small broccoli florets, rinsed
- 2 medium-sized carrots, peeled and thinly-sliced
- 1 small yellow squash, rinsed and thinly-sliced
- 1 red bell pepper, seeded, rinsed and cut into ½-inch squares
- 10 large mushrooms, wiped clean and quartered
- 3 Tb. olive oil
- 1 tsp. dried basil
- 1 tsp. oregano
- 2-3 garlic cloves, peeled and crushed
- 1 tsp. freshly ground black pepper
- ¼ tsp. ground red cayenne pepper (optional)
- ¼ tsp. salt
- ¼ cup unsalted pine nuts or shelled sunflower seeds
- ¼ cup fresh parsley sprigs, chopped
- 4 Tb. grated Parmesan cheese
- ½ lb. provolone cheese, cubed

**1** In large pot, bring 3 quarts of water to boil. Add rotini and follow package directions for al dente cooking time. Drain in colander. Transfer rotini to large serving bowl and drizzle with 1 Tb. olive oil to keep pasta from sticking together. Cover to keep warm.

**2** About 5 minutes before rotini is ready, place broccoli, carrots, squash, red bell pepper and mushrooms in vegetable steamer. Pour 1 inch of water into frying pan and bring to boil at medium-high heat. Place steamer in pan, cover and steam until broccoli is bright green and crisp-tender, 3-4 minutes.

**3** Transfer steamed vegetables to large serving bowl with pasta. Add remaining 2 Tb. olive oil, basil, oregano, black pepper, cayenne pepper and salt. Toss in pine nuts, parsley, Parmesan and provolone cheeses. Mix well to combine, and adjust seasonings to your liking. Serve at once, or cover and chill to serve later.

**Platemates**
Hot Saga Bread (page 82) or Golden Garlic Bread (page 84)

**F.Y.I.**
* Be creative! Add your favorite vegetables or substitute what's in season: asparagus spears, zucchini, green pepper, yellow pepper, water chestnuts (drained), cauliflower florets, snow peas.
* Serve this dish warm or chill and serve later.

**No-Whine Wine Guide**
Full-flavored Chardonnay

# New Wave Lasagna
## Zap it in the microwave—noodles and all! No kidding!

SERVES 6-8

### PrepTime
25 minutes

### CookTime
40 minutes + 10 minutes
standing time

### Pantry Raid
1½-quart microwave-safe
casserole dish with cover,
10"x10"x2" baking dish with
cover (or any large 2 inch-deep
microwave baking dish that fits in
your microwave), large mixing
bowl, spatula

### Grocery Guide
1 lb. lean ground beef
1 16-oz. jar or can spaghetti
    sauce
1 8-oz. can tomato sauce
1 tsp. oregano
2 tsp. freshly ground black pepper
3 garlic cloves, peeled and minced
2 Tb. dried parsley flakes
1 16-oz. container small curd
    cottage cheese
¾ cup grated Parmesan cheese
1 egg
1 tsp. dried basil
8 uncooked lasagna noodles
8 oz. (2 cups) shredded
    mozzarella cheese

### F.Y.I.
✳ For a change of taste, mix
    ½ pound of zesty Italian
    sausage with ½ pound of lean
    ground beef.

**1** Break up ground beef into casserole. Cover loosely and microwave on High (100%) for 3 minutes. Stir. Cover and zap again 2-3 more minutes, or until no pink remains. Drain off fat.

**2** Into beef, stir spaghetti and tomato sauces, oregano, pepper, garlic and 1 Tb. parsley. Cover tightly and nuke on High till sauce bubbles, about 4-5 minutes.

**3** Meanwhile, into mixing bowl add cottage cheese, ½ cup Parmesan cheese, egg, basil and remaining 1 Tb. parsley. Stir till blended.

**4** On bottom of baking dish, evenly spread ⅓ of the meat sauce. Place 4 uncooked lasagna noodles side-by-side over sauce (you may need to break off the ends to fit). Evenly spread half of the cheese mixture and 1 cup mozzarella over noodles. Repeat layering with ⅓ meat sauce, 4 more noodles and remaining cheese mixture (reserve the mozzarella). Top with remaining meat sauce.

**5** Cover tightly and zap on High (100%) for 10 minutes. Rotate dish ½ turn and zap on Medium (50%) another 20-25 minutes, or until noodles are tender. Sprinkle with remaining Parmesan and mozzarella cheeses, cover and let stand 10 minutes before cutting and serving.

---

**No-Whine Wine Guide**
Petite Sirah, Cabernet Sauvignon
    or deep-flavored Italian red

**Platemates**
Golden Garlic Bread (page 84)
    and a garden salad

# Rock 'n' Roll Chicken
## It's got a good taste and you can dance to it.

SERVES 4

**1** Place chicken breasts, one at a time, between 2 sheets of plastic wrap. With a flat mallet or bottom of small saucepan, gently pound until each one is about ¼-inch thick.

**2** In rimmed plate, mix bread crumbs, Parmesan cheese and 3 Tb. chopped parsley. Set aside.

**3** In second rimmed plate, add butter and nuke on **High** (100%) for 1 minute, or till full meltdown. (*Alt:* Melt butter in small saucepan on low heat and pour into rimmed plate.)

**4** Top each chicken breast with a slice of prosciutto and a half-slice of mozzarella. Sprinkle chopped tomatoes and sage equally over all four breasts. Preheat oven to 350º.

**5** Starting at the lower edge of each breast, roll up chicken to enclose filling. Hold the rolled chicken at the seam and dip into melted butter, then into bread crumb mixture till evenly coated. Place coated rolled breasts, seam side down, into baking pan, leaving space between them. Bake, uncovered, 25 minutes, or until chicken is cooked (see Doneness Check). Garnish with remaining 1 Tb. parsley and serve hot!

*Platemates*
Boogie Woogie Broccoli (page 84) and Top 40 Potatoes (page 85)

*No-Whine Wine Guide*
Beaujolais-Villages or Sauvignon Blanc

# CHAPTER 16

# Taming Your Toughest Critics: His Folks

## Win Rave Reviews With These Proven Parent-Pleasers

*t*he experience ranks right in there with sweating out an IRS audit. . .enduring a blind date with a bore. . .and suffering through a root canal.

Having his folks over.

Maybe up till now you were able to hide your inability to cook by showing up with disguised dishes from the deli. By setting the table before dinner. Or by enthusiastically doing the dishes afterwards.

But even if you offer to polish the silver, vacuum the rug or redecorate their rec room, eventually his parents are going to expect you to invite them for dinner.

Well, no problem. Because now you know what it takes to present a masterful meal that even his mother will love. And his father will ask for seconds.

Just view this as an opportunity—not an obligation. Review the tactful tactics and sure-fire parent-pleasers in this chapter. They're all designed to win you critical acclaim from the world's toughest critics.

*Don't miss this opportunity to win brownie points with these powerful allies.*

115

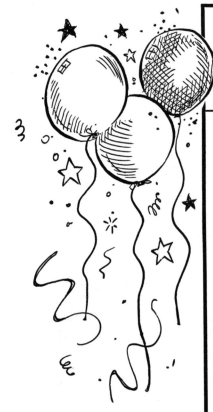

# *good time guide*
## #4:

## *How To Curry Favor With His Folks*

* Mothball your backless cocktail dress and stiletto heels for another occasion. No chandelier earrings. And please. . .don't spike your hair.

* Do not "pre-taste" drinks before the guests arrive, even if you're a nervous wreck. Better to be a bit on edge than way over the edge.

* Don't get drawn into family arguments. And no debates with their "baby" until his folks leave.

* No ethnic jokes, political barbs or off-color humor—no matter how crude *he* gets.

* Graciously turn the other cheek if they slip and call you by his ex's name.

* Freely drop comments that you see where he gets his (a) good looks (b) fine manners (c) ambition (d) intelligence (e) creativity (f) _____
  (fill in positive trait here)

* Work your personal and career accomplishments into the conversation. But stop short of bragging about your bigger salary, faster car or beach-front condo.

# Quickie Quiche
*Real men like it, too.*

**PrepTime**
20 minutes

**CookTime**
60 minutes

**Pantry Raid**
Frying pan, medium-sized mixing bowl

**Grocery Guide**
1 Tb. butter
½ medium onion, peeled and finely chopped
5 oz. broccoli florets, cut small
1 ready-made deep-dish pie shell in 9-inch aluminum pie pan
12 medium-sized fresh mushrooms, wiped clean and sliced
½ cup grated sharp cheddar cheese
½ cup grated Monterey Jack cheese

*For egg mixture:*
3 eggs
¼ cup milk
½ cup whipping cream
¼ tsp. ground white pepper
¼ tsp. nutmeg
Pinch of salt

**Platemates**
Marvelous Mandarin Salad (page 53), French bread

**No-Whine Wine Guide**
Chardonnay or Mâcon-Villages

**1** Preheat oven to 450º.

**2** In frying pan on low heat, melt butter, tilting pan to coat bottom. Add onion and sauté until translucent, about 3-4 minutes. Add broccoli florets and sauté 3 minutes more. Remove pan from heat and set aside.

**3** Into bowl add eggs, milk, cream, white pepper, nutmeg and salt. Stir with fork till blended.

**4** Into pie crust, add broccoli, onions, mushrooms, cheddar and Monterey Jack cheeses. Pour egg mixture over the top and lightly arrange with fork.

**5** Place in center of oven and bake 15 minutes. Reduce heat to 350º and bake 45 minutes more or till done (see Doneness Check). Remove from oven and let cool 10 minutes before serving.

**F.Y.I.**
* *Quiche Doneness Check:* When knife inserted in center of quiche comes out clean, it's ready.
* For a European flair, substitute Swiss and Gruyere cheese for the cheddar and Monterey Jack.
* Save time and money by picking up broccoli florets at the salad bar.

117

# *A*pple Pocket Pork Chops
## *Swiped from Granny's secret file.*

*PrepTime*
15 minutes

*CookTime*
40 minutes

*Pantry Raid*
Medium-sized saucepan, 9"x13" baking pan, chef's knife, tongs

*Grocery Guide*
1 Tb. butter or margarine
½ small yellow onion, finely chopped
½ Granny Smith apple, skin on, cored and diced
⅔ cup apple sauce
2 Tb. raisins
4 pork chops, cut 1-inch thick
4 Tb. honey mustard
¼ cup plain dried bread crumbs
Freshly ground black pepper

*Platemates*
The Wildest Rice You Ever Ate (page 87), steamed broccoli

*F.Y.I.*
* If you can't find honey mustard, mix 2 Tb. honey and 2 Tb. mustard.
* *Pork Doneness Check:* When meat near bone is no longer pink when slashed with a knife.
* Ask your friendly butcher to cut the chops 1-inch thick for you.

*No-Whine Wine Guide*
Riesling or Vouvray

**1** *Make the stuffing:* In saucepan, melt butter on medium heat and sauté onions 2 minutes. Add diced apple and sauté 2 minutes more. Mix in apple sauce and raisins, bring to a boil and stir for 3 minutes. Reduce heat to low and simmer mixture 10 minutes, stirring occasionally.

**2** Meanwhile, with chef's knife, slice horizontally through each chop to form a deep pocket. Set aside.

**3** Coat bottom of baking pan with 2 Tb. honey mustard—reserve the rest to coat chops. Then preheat oven to 400º.

**4** Carefully stuff chops with hot apple mixture and place in single layer in baking pan. Coat top of chops with remaining 2 Tb. honey mustard and sprinkle with bread crumbs and pepper.

**5** Bake 35-40 minutes, or till done (see Doneness Check). Serve immediately!

# $\mathcal{S}$tuffed Pasta Perfecto
## The perfect way to stuff your parents, too.

---

**PrepTime**
35 minutes

**CookTime**
30 minutes

**Pantry Raid**
Large pot, colander, frying pan, medium-sized mixing bowl, large casserole dish with cover
(or 9"x 13" baking pan and aluminum foil to cover)

**Grocery Guide**
20 jumbo macaroni shells (buy the 12 oz. box)

*For meat sauce:*
2 Tb. olive oil
¾ lb. lean ground beef
½ medium-sized yellow onion, peeled and finely chopped
2 cloves garlic, peeled and minced
16 oz. zesty tomato sauce
6 oz. can tomato paste
½ tsp. oregano
½ tsp. basil
¼ tsp. freshly ground black pepper
¼ tsp. salt

*For cheese mixture:*
1 egg
1 cup cottage cheese
½ cup shredded mozzarella cheese
3 Tb. rinsed and finely chopped fresh parsley sprigs

**No-Whine Wine Guide**
Côtes du Rhône, or deep-red Zinfandel

**1** In large pot, boil water and add 20 unbroken shells. Follow package directions for al dente cooking time. Drain in colander and set aside.

**2** Meanwhile, in frying pan on medium heat, heat 1 Tb. olive oil and add ground beef, stirring to break up meat. Cook till no pink remains, about 4 minutes. Drain off fat and transfer meat to clean plate.

**3** Add remaining 1 Tb. olive oil to frying pan on medium heat and sauté onions till golden (4-5 minutes). Reduce heat to low, return meat to pan and stir in garlic, tomato sauce, tomato paste, oregano, basil, pepper and salt. Mix thoroughly and simmer uncovered for 10 minutes, stirring occasionally.

**4** Meanwhile, in mixing bowl, beat egg lightly and stir in cottage cheese, mozzarella cheese and parsley. Preheat oven to 350°. Lightly oil the bottom and sides of casserole dish. Spread ¼ of the meat sauce on the bottom, and arrange cooked shells in single layer, open-side up.

**5** Stuff each shell halfway with remaining meat sauce, then fill to top with cheese sauce (or alternate cheese/meat sauce for visual variety). Cover, place casserole in center of oven and bake 20 minutes. Remove cover and bake 5 minutes more. With spatula, transfer stuffed shells to dinner plates and garnish with fresh sprigs of parsley.

# CHAPTER 17

# Let's Do Munch

## Cook Your Way To The Top With These Potluck Prizewinners

Sooner or later, you'll have to produce more than big profits for your company, give more than gifts at bridal and baby showers, or bring more than your smiling face to holiday dinners.

Yes, we're talking "potluck." And after you've mastered this chapter, your only specialties won't be napkins, ice or beer anymore. (Only men and chief execs can get away with that.)

Just keep in mind that in every office gang, party crowd and family reunion lurk a few gluttons. So you can be sure that any culinary creation—no matter how ghastly—will eventually be consumed. You hope.

But now you're aiming for the incredible, not the merely edible. You want to hear more than, "Golly, that was really...*filling*." Or, "Oh, that looks so...*interesting*." Or even, "Gee, you really shouldn't have...."

Now you'll get comments like, "You *must* give me the recipe!" And, "You're so successful...and you can cook, too!" Or even, "This is so fabulous, I'm going to:

- give you a promotion and a raise!
- give you half my shower gifts!
- transfer you to our Paris office!"

Despite what you might think, a career and cooking are not mutually exclusive. And now you'll be able to cook your way to the top.

121

# Jambalaya Jumble
## *Me-oh-my-oh!*

*PrepTime*
30 minutes

*CookTime*
50 minutes

*Pantry Raid*
3 quart (or larger) oven-to-range-top casserole dish with cover, oven mitts

*Grocery Guide*
2 Tb. vegetable oil
½ lb. hot Italian sausage or Kielbasa, cut into ¼-inch pieces
½ lb. smoked unsliced ham steak, cut into ½-inch cubes
1 lb. boneless, skinless chicken breasts, cut into ½-inch cubes
1 large red bell pepper, seeded, rinsed and coarsely chopped
4 garlic cloves, peeled and minced
8 green onions (bulb plus green), sliced
1 cup uncooked converted white rice
1 (1 lb., 12 oz.) can tomatoes, not drained
1 tsp. salt
½ tsp. freshly ground black pepper
½ tsp. red cayenne pepper
1 Tb. parsley flakes
1 pound medium-sized shrimp, peeled and deveined

*No-Whine Wine Guide*
Gewürztraminer or beer

**1** On rangetop over medium-low heat, heat oil in casserole dish. Add sausage and ham and stir till lightly browned on all sides, about 5 minutes. Drain off fat. Add chicken, green pepper, garlic and onions and stir 3 minutes more.

**2** Reduce heat to low, add rice and stir for 5 minutes. Preheat oven to 350º.

**3** Stir in tomatoes, breaking up any large pieces, salt, black pepper, red pepper, parsley and 1 cup water. Increase heat to medium-high and stir occasionally till mixture comes to a boil. Remove from heat and cover. With oven mitts, place casserole in center of oven and bake for 20 minutes.

**4** Stir mixture and add shrimp, pushing them down into the hot mixture. Add a little water if mixture seems dry. Continue baking 15 minutes more, taste and adjust seasonings and serve in bowls.

*Platemates*
Hot buttered French bread, Strong-To-The-Finish Spinach Salad (page 54—double or triple the ingredients as needed)

*F.Y.I.*
∗ Prepare Jambalaya Jumble a day in advance—just cover tightly and refrigerate. To serve, bring to room temperature and reheat in a 300º oven till hot, about 20 minutes, or zap in microwave on High (100%) for 5 minutes, stir, and zap again for 3-4 minutes or till hot.
∗ If you can find yellow rice, substitute 1 cup (2-five ounce packages) for the white rice.

# Hearty Veggie Medley
## Tastes great. . .and it's good for you!

**PrepTime**
20 minutes

**CookTime**
7 minutes

**Pantry Raid**
Deep pot with cover, vegetable steamer that fits into pot, large serving bowl, plastic wrap, jar with tight-fitting lid

**Grocery Guide**
½ lb. green beans, rinsed, ends trimmed and cut into 1-inch pieces
2 cups bite-sized cauliflower florets, rinsed
2 medium-sized carrots, peeled and cut into ¼-inch coins
2 cups bite-sized broccoli florets, rinsed
1 medium-sized zucchini, rinsed, ends trimmed and cut into ½-inch coins
1 red bell pepper, seeded, rinsed and cut into thin 1-inch-long strips

*For the dressing:*
⅓ cup red wine vinegar
2 garlic cloves, peeled and minced
2 green onions (bulb plus 2 inches green), chopped
½ tsp. salt
½ tsp. red cayenne pepper
1 Tb. parsley flakes
½ tsp. oregano
½ tsp. dried basil
2 tsp. sugar
2 Tb. Dijon mustard
⅔ cup olive or other salad oil

**1** *At least 45 minutes ahead of time:* Pour 1 inch of water into deep pot and bring to boil at medium-high heat.

**2** Into vegetable steamer add green beans, cauliflower and carrots. Place steamer in pot, cover and steam vegetables 4 minutes.

**3** Add broccoli and zucchini to steamer, cover, and steam 3 minutes more.

**4** With oven mitt, remove steamer from pot and rinse vegetables well under cold running water. Shake off all excess water and transfer vegetables to large serving bowl. Add red bell pepper, cover with plastic wrap and refrigerate till vegetables are chilled, 30 minutes or more.

**5** *Make the dressing:* Into jar add the red wine vinegar, garlic, green onions, salt, cayenne pepper, parsley flakes, oregano, sugar, mustard and oil. Cap tightly and shake well. *When ready to serve:* Shake dressing well, pour over vegetables and toss to coat.

**Platemates**
Golden Garlic Bread (page 84)
**No-Whine Wine Guide**
Chardonnay or Pouilly-Fuissé

**F.Y.I.**
✱ Add dressing to salad up to 1 hour before serving, and serve at room temperature.

# CHAPTER 18

# Beauty & The Beasts

### How To Stuff Your Wild Party Animals

Would you like to play hostess to a cheering crowd... satisfy their robust appetites...and pay back all those party invitations you owe?

Then host a Hearty Party at your place. A Gang Shebang. Gorgy. Beast Feast. Birthday Blow-Out. Or celebrate that new job, new home, new baby...or recent divorce.

And if you'd really like to score points with your beau, throw a Pigskin Pig-Out or a Baseball Belly-Buster. You'll impress his buddies, light up the scoreboard and gather eligible bachelors in your living room for close inspection by your single girlfriends.

Just follow these guidelines from the sidelines to turn your next scrimmage into a Superbowl...gain the home-field advantage...and tackle the job without a fumble.

*Roll-up the Persian rug, anchor down the antiques and toss a tarp over the couch so you can enjoy the party, too!*

125

# *good time guide* #5:

## *Score Big With These Tips From The Pros*

* Know who's playing. Wear team colors. If you start getting drowsy, silently play "Rate the Rear Ends."

* Don't show the game on your Sony Watchman. Borrow a wide-screen TV.

* Add color to your buffet with seasonal or topical centerpieces. Try flowers, holly berries, gourds, balloons, your old cheerleader pom-poms. . . . But avoid footballs; the jocks are sure to chuck them around your living room.

* Put your Ming vase and other valuables out of reach. Just pretend you're having the local day care kids over for kickball practice.

* Give yourself a break. Don't play bartender—appoint one. Or set up a self-serve bar in an easily accessible place.

* Get hoorays for your buffets. Keep hot food hot and cold food cold.

* Don't serve messy foods unless you want your meal immortalized on your designer furniture.

* Scatter stacks of napkins in easy-to-see-and-reach places. And have plenty of paper towels on hand for accidents. (We're talking cases, not rolls.)

* Use sturdy paper plates and strong plastic utensils to cut clean-up time.

* Dieting? Give doggie bags to your friends. Or freeze leftovers so you're not tempted to clean out the fridge every time you go for a diet cola.

* Need a Post-Party Hangover Cure? Dissolve ten cases of Alka-Seltzer in the bath tub.

# *H*ot Sausage Superheroes
## *Goes great with hot buns.*

*PrepTime*
8 minutes

*CookTime*
45 minutes

*Pantry Raid*
Large pot, large frying pan with cover, spatula, tongs

*Grocery Guide*
4 hot or mild Italian sausage links (about ⅓ lb. each)
2 Tb. olive oil
1 green bell pepper, seeded, rinsed and cut into 2-inch-long strips
1 red bell pepper, seeded, rinsed and cut into 2-inch-long strips
1 medium-sized red onion, peeled, halved and cut into thin strips
3 plum tomatoes, rinsed and diced
¼ cup red wine
½ tsp. freshly ground black pepper
1 tsp. oregano
4 fresh Italian sub rolls

*Platemates*
Corn on the cob or corn niblets, store-bought potato salad and green salad

*No-Whine Wine Guide*
Gewürztraminer—or beer!

**1** Half-fill large pot with water and bring to boil at high heat. Reduce heat to medium, add sausages and simmer 15 minutes. Remove sausages from water with tongs.

**2** Meanwhile, add olive oil to frying pan on medium heat. Add green and red peppers and onions and sauté 6-7 minutes.

**3** Stir tomatoes and wine into frying pan. Increase heat to high until most of the liquid has boiled off, about 10 minutes. Stir occasionally.

**4** Reduce heat to low, add sausages and season with pepper and oregano. Cover for about 25 minutes, turning the sausages a few times. Sausage is ready when there are no traces of pink through cut in center.

**5** Cut rolls lengthwise and place one sausage in each. Smother with vegetable mixture and serve hot!

*F.Y.I.*

∗ Double the proportions and use two frying pans to serve eight sports fans.

∗ Warm the rolls for a few minutes in your oven at 250º before Step 5.
∗ Reduce the fat by using turkey sausage (and don't tell 'em!)

# Superbowlful of Chili
## The dinner of champions!

### PrepTime
10 minutes
### CookTime
1-1½ hours
### Pantry Raid
5 quart pot, working can opener, grater

### Grocery Guide
2 medium-sized yellow onions, peeled and coarsely chopped
2 Tb. vegetable oil
1¼ pound lean ground beef
1 can (1 lb. 12 oz.) tomatoes, not drained
1 can (1 lb. 11 oz.) red kidney beans, not drained
1 Tb. chili powder
3-4 garlic cloves, peeled and crushed
2 tsp. oregano leaves
½ tsp. cumin
¾ tsp. salt
1 Tb. cider vinegar

*For the garnish:*
4 oz. sharp cheddar cheese, grated
1 medium-sized yellow onion, coarsely chopped

### No-Whine Wine Guide
Ice-cold beer, lightly chilled Côtes du Rhône or wine coolers.

**1** Heat oil in large pot over medium heat. Add onions and stir-fry 8-10 minutes or until golden.

**2** Add ground beef, breaking up with spatula and stirring until meat turns completely from red to brown, 4-5 minutes. Carefully drain and discard hot fat from pot.

**3** Stir in tomatoes and juices, breaking up tomatoes as you stir. Then stir in kidney beans and liquid, chili powder, garlic, oregano, cumin, salt and cider vinegar. Mix thoroughly.

**4** Simmer at low heat, uncovered, for at least 45 minutes—and up to 1½ hours if possible. Stir occasionally.

**5** Place grated cheddar and chopped raw onions in two bowls and serve!

### Platemates
Avocado wedges, fresh tortilla chips and corn bread
### F.Y.I.
* For three-alarm chili, add ⅛ tsp. crushed hot red chili peppers 10 minutes before mixture is finished simmering.
* Serve with two bowls of chopped raw onion and grated cheddar cheese for guests to top their chili.

# CONGRATULATIONS!

## Post-Graduate Studies

Just think...now you can whip up masterful meals for your mate, friends, parents—even in-laws! To help you cope with your future cooking challenges, just turn to the following food for thought. Good luck!

# How to Cheat (Without Getting Caught)

## Sometimes You Just Gotta Fake It

*h*e'll be there in less than half an hour. . . and you just got out of a morning meeting that lasted all day. What do you do now? Make a quick stop at your local market on the way home and pick up the items you need for one of these tasty short-cuts below.

If he asks if it's homemade, just say "yes." (But don't tell him *whose* home.) And be sure to dispose of labeled boxes, cans and other evidence before serving. You don't want the cardboard base of your store-bought cake to reveal the shocking truth!

* ***Jiffy dip:*** Into a cup of sour cream, mix sliced green onions, fresh parsley, dill or other herbs. Serve with fresh chips.

* ***Soup-er dip:*** Buy dry vegetable soup mix and follow the easy directions for the dip.

* ***Fast 'n' festive salads:*** Harvest the salad bar at your local grocery store.

* ***Dressed-up dressing:*** Pour your favorite salad dressing in a dish, top with fresh parsley and freshly ground pepper.

* ***Uncanny soup:*** Garnish canned soup with chopped parsley and/or grated Parmesan cheese.

* ***Almost-homemade pasta sauce:*** Buy a jar of thick ready-to-serve tomato sauce. Add some chunks of fresh steamed vegetables, garlic, parsley and serve over hot pasta.

* ***Ice dream:*** Top your favorite ice cream with fresh fruit and top with 1/2 oz. of liqueur.

* ***Easy sweet:*** Stroll down to your local bakery and pick up a few good-looking pastries. Toss box, base, receipt and indulge!

* ***No-bake cheesecake:*** Top a ready-made cheesecake with fresh or frozen (and thawed) strawberries or blueberries.

# Feast Aid

*Try these quick fixes before you call for carry-out:*

* **Too much spice?** Multiply other ingredients to match proportion (within reason).
* **Too thick?** Add water or milk.
* **Too thin?** Add 1 Tb. cornstarch pre-dissolved in 1 Tb. of water.
* **Too greasy?** Skim lettuce leaves or ice cubes across the surface.
* **Salt shaker clogged?** Add a few grains of rice to prevent clumping.
* **Clumpy brown sugar?** Heat it briefly over very low heat or in the microwave.
* **Garlic or onion fingers?** Rub 'em with lemon juice.
* **Too far gone?** Whip out a girl's best friend (the American Excess card).

## Tastes Great—Less Fattening

* **Sleeker pans and bodies:** Use non-stick pan-coating sprays to cut calories and clean-up time. Do *not* use hairspray.
* **Slimmer soup:** Cut calories by substituting whole milk for cream and half-and-half.
* **Leaner cuisine:** Substitute low-fat plain yogurt for sour cream.
* **Naturally sweet:** Instead of sugar and low-cal chemical sweeteners, try fruit juices, cinnamon and nutmeg. Not hot fudge.
* **Avoid sodium OD's:** Go light on salt and soy sauce.

# Vital Statistics

*Remember these
equivalents, conversions
and kitchen whiz-dom*

1/8 tsp. garlic powder = 1 garlic clove
1 lemon = 2-3 Tb. lemon juice
1 cup uncooked rice = 3 cups cooked
1 cup cookie crumbs = 0 calories

1 pinch = 1/8 tsp.
3 tsp. = 1 Tb.
2 Tb. = 1 fluid oz.
4 Tb. = 1/4 cup
1 cup = 8 fluid oz.
2 cups = 1 pint
1 pint ice cream = 2 lb. cellulite

1 oz. = 28.35 grams
16 oz. = 1 lb.
1 stick butter = 8 Tb.
1 stick butter = 1/2 cup melted
1 pound butter = 1 pair love handles

4 oz. firm cheese = 1 cup shredded
3 oz. hard cheese = ½ cup grated
6 oz. chocolate chips = 1 cup
1 cup chocolate chips = 1" (per thigh)

# Keeping It Fresh

*Like Most Men, The Foods You Buy Require Watchful Eyes*

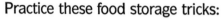

Practice these food storage tricks:

* *Fruit:* It's harvested and shipped while green, so buy in advance and allow to ripen at room temperature. If it turns green again, throw it out.

* *Vegetables:* Refrigerate in vegetable compartment to prevent over-ripening. Keep dry; allow air to circulate. Store mushrooms in a paper bag.

* *Eggs:* If the egg sinks in a bowl of cold water, it's still fresh. If it floats, toss it at your ex's car.

* *Cheese:* Wrap tightly in plastic. Air hardens it into a great doorstop. It's best to buy fresh for each meal.

* *Cooking oils:* Store in a cool, dark place—your night table drawer, for instance.

* *Garlic:* Place in glass jar, puncture lid and store in the refrigerator.

* *Fresh Herbs:* Preserve in a covered jar by submerging stems in an inch of water and refrigerating.

* *Chocolate:* Store in a cool, dark, dry place. Don't refrigerate; it'll discolor. (Chocoholics: store at a trusted friend's.)

* *Meat:* Rewrap in plastic (not foil) and store in the coldest part of your fridge, up to 4 days. Freezing changes the texture, so it's best to buy fresh.

* *Fish:* Catch it yourself or buy it fresh. You can rewrap and refrigerate up to 3 days. If it smells fishy, toss it overboard.

* *Poultry:* Lasts only one to two days in the fridge, but 6 months in the freezer. Rewrap by the piece in plastic or freezer paper.

* *Bread:* Wrap in plastic and keep dry. If you freeze it, allow it to thaw for up to 8 hours, then crisp in a 375° oven for 2 minutes. Don't trash stale bread—make croutons or toast, unless it's green and fuzzy.

* *Leftovers:* Refrigerate or freeze immediately.

# Granny's Secrets Revealed

*Sneak A Peak At Her Confidential Techniques*

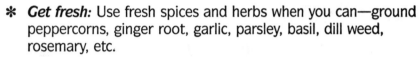

* ***Get fresh:*** Use fresh spices and herbs when you can—ground peppercorns, ginger root, garlic, parsley, basil, dill weed, rosemary, etc.

* ***Ripen up:*** To ripen tomatoes, stick them in a paper bag with an apple.

* ***Get juiced:*** Squeeze more juice from your lemon by microwaving 20 seconds on High (100%).

* ***Butter 'em up:*** Sauté vegetables in a little butter before mixing with other ingredients; make their flavor blossom.

* ***Put a halt to salt:*** Cut back with these substitutes: spices, herbs, garlic, green onion, citrus fruit, juices, vinegar, wine.

* ***Try a little tenderness:*** If you use salt, don't add it until you're nearly done cooking. Salt toughens some foods.

* ***Eggceptional eggs:*** Let eggs come to room temperature and cook them over low-medium heat to keep 'em fluffy.

* ***Avoid stuck-up pasta:*** Add a pat of butter or margarine or 1 Tb. of cooking oil to boiling water.

* ***Great buns:*** Heat your fresh bread and rolls wrapped in foil at 300° for 4–5 minutes. But don't microwave or they'll get soggy. And let butter come to room temperature before serving. (No squeeze bottles of margarine or mustard on the table—wait till you're married.)

* ***Dazzle 'em:*** Serve chilled, sparkling bottled water in wine glasses. Garnish with a wedge of lemon.

* ***No pain, no stain:***
    RED WINE STAINS—rub in salt, dunk in cold water and scrub. Or, just tie-dye the whole tablecloth.
    FRUIT STAINS—stretch stained area across a bowl and pour boiling water through the stain.
    GREASE STAINS—try club soda.
    ALCOHOL STAINS—soak immediately in cold water and a little glycerine, then rinse with white vinegar and water.

135

# SOS—Save Our Suppers

*Dinner's Not The Time To Cash In On Your Health or Fire Insurance*

* **Burnin' down the house:** For a fire in a pan, quickly clap a lid on it and move it to the sink. You can also extinguish fires with handfuls of baking soda. Never use water or flour! It's smart to keep a working smoke detector and fire extinguisher nearby (buy a Class ABC with a 2A minimum capacity). Don't be inducted into the Hall of Flame.

* **Ohhhh. . .that's HOT!** Always wear oven mitts or use pot holders to pull out the oven rack and to handle red-hot dishes. In case of minor burns, keep a well-stocked first-aid kit, and apply ice cubes to prevent blisters. Or grow an aloe plant and apply the liquid inside a leaf to the burn.

* **Why is the utility bill so high?** Turn off all appliances, oven and burners as soon as you're done cooking.

* **Tips from a pan-handler:** Always position pan handles so you won't accidentally tip hot liquids onto clothes, shoes and wide-eyed pets. But don't turn them over other hot burners where they'll melt, either. And be sure to tighten all wobbly handles.

* ***Stop belly-achin':*** Prevent food poisoning—never use the same dishes or utensils to prepare and serve meat without washing them thoroughly between steps. Defrost food only in the refrigerator. Refrigerate leftovers at once. And don't use cans that bulge or contain odd-smelling food (no taste tests!).

* ***Half-baked advice:*** Make sure you thoroughly cook pork (till it's white throughout) and chicken (till it's completely white and juices run clear).

* ***Some cutting remarks:*** Always use extreme care when handling knives. And don't lose sight of them under soapy dish water.

* ***If your oven's running a fever:*** To check the accuracy of your oven heat, place an oven thermometer on rack in center of oven, set the temperature knob, wait 10 minutes and check reading. Adjust the knob if necessary.

* ***Time is on your side:*** Keep an eye on the clock or use a timer. Remember, just a couple of moments separate Spaghetti Carbonara from Carbonized Spaghetti.

# Know Your A-B-Seasonings

*These Handy Illustrated Techniques Will Help You Look As Good As You Cook.*

## Mincing & Crushing Garlic

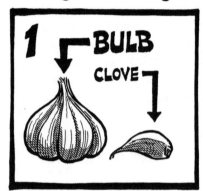

**1** BULB CLOVE

Memorize the difference between a bulb and a clove of garlic (or you'll scare off fleas, ticks, vampires—and your date!).

**2**

Lightly crush clove under the broad side of a knife. Peel all papery wrapping from around clove until you reach the smooth, shiny flesh.

**3**

Mince clove or crush in garlic press. Or save yourself all the trouble and buy one of those 4 oz. jars of pre-crushed or pre-minced garlic in citric acid.

## Preparing Green Onions

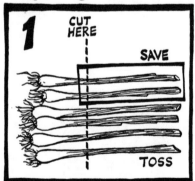

**1** CUT HERE SAVE TOSS

Trim leafy tops off green onions (a/k/a spring onions or scallions) 2 inches from bulb. (Save two tops for use as an easy dinner plate garnish.)

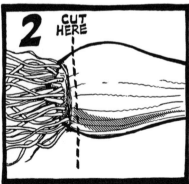

**2** CUT HERE

Slice off the roots.

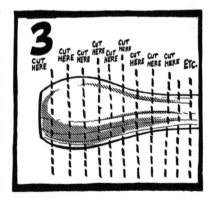

**3** CUT HERE CUT HERE CUT HERE CUT HERE CUT HERE CUT HERE CUT HERE CUT HERE CUT HERE ETC.

Peel off outer layer of onion and slice remaining bulb into disks. Now you're cookin'!

## Preparing Shrimp

 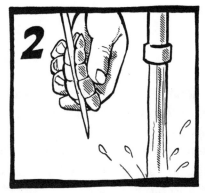 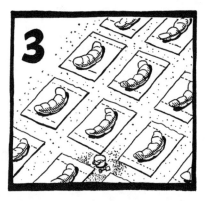

To shell raw shrimp, remove the legs, then split the shell open down the center of the shrimp. Hold the tail and gently pull the shell away from the body of the shrimp.

Remove black sand vein by making a shallow cut along the entire length of the shrimp's back with a paring knife. Rinse it out under cold water.

Set shrimp to dry on paper towels, and refrigerate if preparing shrimp ahead of time.

## Preparing Mushrooms

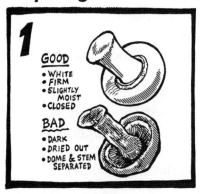  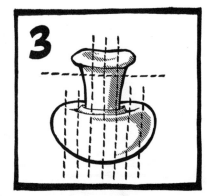

Buy only fresh mushrooms.

Use a dampened paper towel or cloth to wipe dirt and grit off mushrooms.

Trim off bottom of stem. If recipe requires, cut lengthwise along dotted lines about ⅛-inch thick.

# Glossary

*Learn how to crack the cryptic code of cooking terms.*

cube

dice

mince

sauté

**Al dente** Pasta cooked until tender but slightly firm to the bite.

**Baste** To brush or spoon pan drippings or other liquid over food as it cooks.

**Blend** To thoroughly mix ingredients until smooth.

**Chop** To cut food into small pieces, coarser than minced.

**Coat** To dip in crumbs, flour or other dry ingredient.

**Cube** To cut food into half-inch cubes.

**Dash** Less than ⅛ teaspoon.

**Dice** To cut food into fine cubes about ⅛th inch.

**Drizzle** To pour liquid slowly over food in a fine stream.

**Dust** To sprinkle lightly with flour or sugar.

**Flambé** To ignite liquor-drenched foods.

**Floret** The small heads of broccoli or cauliflower.

**Grate** To shred food into small particles.

**Marinate** To steep food in a savory liquid till food absorbs its flavor

**Mince** To cut or chop into very fine particles.

**Pith** The bitter white area surrounding sections of citrus fruit.

**Preheat** To bring oven or frying pan to desired temperature before adding food.

**Sauté** To fry quickly in a pan while stirring continuously.

**Score** To cut shallow grooves in outer layer of food.

**Shred** To cut or grate into thin, irregular strips.

**Simmer** To cook liquid over low heat just below boiling.

**Whisk** To beat with a wire whisk or fork till blended.

**Zest** Outer colored peel of citrus fruits.

# The Ultimate Compliment

*"He's wonderful and good looking. Problem is—he can't cook. Get him EATING IN, which . . .will turn a bumbling bachelor into a master chef."* —PLAYGIRL

**Now available in your local bookstore. Or use this coupon to order.**

*"Now there's help for the guy who wants to give that special woman a unique gift—a home-cooked meal. It's in a paperback book called EATING IN."*

—Associated Press Newsfeatures

# Even The Score!
## And wake up the flavor in relationships.

Don't let him think your newfound culinary skills mean he can expect regular feedings every time his stomach growls. Here's the sure-fire way to break this unappetizing habit:

Get him a copy of *EATING IN—The Official Single Man's Cookbook—* the real man's illustrated guide to "home-cooked romance" (Miami *Herald*) that's "witty and wise" (PLAYBOY) and "funny and sexy" (Baltimore *Sun*).

Now he'll find out how easily he can dazzle you with dinners like Shrimp Scampi and Chicken Marsala. Pour the wine that's a winner with dinner. And even clean the entire house!

Imagine . . . now you can get him to prepare tantalizing gourmet dinners expressly for you—while you relax and sip fine wine. Give him a copy of *EATING IN*. It's like buying a marvelous gift for yourself!

# How To Turn The Tables On This:

Achieve equal rights in the kitchen with "Mr. Feed-Me-Now."
Hand him *EATING IN — The Official Single Man's Cookbook*!
See page 143 to order.